JUN 11 2008

RAINBOW

PINK LADIES

—&—

CRIMSON GENTS

Portraits and Legends of 50 Roses

MOLLY *and* DON GLENTZER

CLARKSON POTTER/PUBLISHERS
NEW YORK

Library of Congress Cataloging-in-Publication
Data
Glentzer, Molly, 1956–
    Pink ladies & crimson gents / Molly
and Don Glentzer. — 1st ed.
Includes index.
    1. Roses—Varieties.   2. Roses—Varieties—
Anecdotes.   I. Glentzer, Don.   II. Title.
SB411.6.G54   2008
635.9'33734—dc22   2007014926

ISBN 978–0–307–35273–6

Printed in China

Design by Laura Palese

10 9 8 7 6 5 4 3 2 1

First Edition

to the memory of our mothers

Contents

INTRODUCTION
9

CHAPTER 1
ARTFUL PERSONALITIES
12

CHAPTER 2
HEROES & HEROINES
36

CHAPTER 3
NOBLES & NOTABLES
62

CHAPTER 4
STORIED CHARACTERS
88

CHAPTER 5
WELL-BRED LADIES & GENTS
110

ACKNOWLEDGMENTS 136
GROWING OLD-FASHIONED ROSES 137
RESOURCES 139   FURTHER READING 140   INDEX 143

Introduction

THIS BOOK BEGAN WITH A WOMAN IN A BLUE BATHROBE. She was nothing like art's much-referenced Olympia, reclining on a divan in dim light. Her name was Martha Gonzales, and she lived in the sleepy little town of Navasota, Texas.

In a photograph that once appeared in Antique Rose Emporium catalogs, Martha stood at the rickety back steps to her modest frame house beside a scruffy rosebush—an old red China, long out of commerce. It's what preservationists call a "found" rose. And since they rediscovered it at Martha's back door, they named it after her.

Well past middle age, with a shiny gray coif, Martha posed for the photograph in a quilted polyester bathrobe with a Peter Pan collar, buttoned from top to bottom, that fell just below her knees. It bulged slightly, a red sweatshirt peeking out from under the sleeves. She wore utilitarian shoes and white stockings of the sort doctors recommend for better blood circulation. Squinting in the sun behind large glasses, she was not smiling.

Mike Shoup, the Antique Rose Emporium's owner, remembers Martha as generous and warmhearted. But in that picture she looked a little stern, and her namesake rose has proven to be a tough old broad, too. The seven 'Martha Gonzales' bushes out by the street in front of my house are like a thorny chorus line: They have been submerged in smelly floodwater and run over by trucks, but they keep kicking.

Elsewhere in my smallish urban garden are Antique Roses that are also hardy but whose names evoke something entirely different—prominence, propriety, and romance. Yet until I began researching this book, most of the characters these roses honor were a mystery. Who, I kept wondering, was the *real* 'Lady Banks'? The real 'Duchesse de Brabant'?

I assumed whoever introduced these roses years ago would have explained how the names came about, offering some version of a 'Martha Gonzales' portrait in their catalogs. Well. Picture Alice tumbling down a rabbit hole, into the fascinating but relatively uncharted territory where horticulture and human culture collide. It didn't escape me that a book by J. H. Nicholas, written in 1937, was called *A Rose Odyssey*.

"The history of roses is the history of humanity," Nicholas wrote. The fifty Old Rose figures I describe include a sampling of the many "human" types out there, somewhere, with their feet in the mulch—fictional characters, artists, aristocrats, heroes, and plantsmen. To learn who these people were—and discover how roses came to be named for them—I compared historical events and rose introduction dates, sifted through dozens of old, often out-of-print books, and talked to experts. I also had to relearn history I'd forgotten since college—sorting out all the King Louies and such. But not all early hybridizers kept meticulous records, and many records that were kept have since been lost. The full names of some important breeders are a mystery. As it turns out, even experts often read between the lines when they play the rose name game.

Roses have been cultivated for thousands of years, although the practice of naming them for people didn't begin in earnest until the nineteenth century, when European breeders, often using species arriving from China, began pollinating plants artificially to develop new varieties. France was the center of this activity—which accounts for the abundance of roses whose names begin with 'Madame' and 'Monsieur'.

One of the first named roses, 'Grand Napoléon', was a no-brainer. Empress Joséphine Bonaparte, Napoléon's fashionable first wife, patronized many nurserymen and collected every known variety of rose—about 250 at the time—for her estate at Malmaison. By the late 1820s, the number of cultivars had quadrupled, to about 1,000. (To put perspective on the issue, about 14,000 cultivars are believed to exist today.)

The great hybridizer Jean-Pierre Vibert—who got his start by rescuing thousands of seedlings after one of Joséphine's gardeners fled to Russia—foresaw that by its name alone, a rose could provide a living lesson in history and culture as well as inspire the imagination. Thus, in his 1824 *Essay on Roses,* the patriotic Vibert encouraged fellow hybridizers to select names honoring French heroes and "virtuous citizens," characters from classical literature, and—if a rose was delicately colored—"the amiable sex." While he admitted it was "often very difficult to find names which are truly appropriate," he thought a rose's name, when possible, should relate to the plant's appearance.

But raising roses was expensive—even today, it takes several years to develop a new cultivar—and nurserymen who were less fastidious than Vibert happily obliged bourgeois patrons who fancied seeing a little of themselves in the garden or wanted to remember lost loved ones with a token legacy. Confusion ensued when "good" names were duplicated on multiple roses of varying quality. Well into the twentieth century, a single rose might also have multiple identities—because names have a huge influence on a rose's marketability. Take two of the best-selling roses in American history, for example, which originated in France: 'Madame Ferdinand Jamin' became 'American Beauty' here, and 'Madame Antoine Meilland' became 'Peace'.

My husband, photographer Don Glentzer, was absorbed by the possibilities of bringing roses to life on film. The images he created for each story are a photographic interpretation of classic botanical illustrations. Looking at them as I wrote, I set my fancy free—reflecting on their appearance, looking for connections to the stories of their namesakes. (I especially love the rogues among them.) I hope you'll let your imagination wander, too—after all, isn't that what armchair gardening is about?

It's always a pleasure to view something familiar with a fresh eye. In juxtaposing Don's photographs with the stories, I discovered that these roses and their human counterparts actually do share some characteristics. For rose fanciers like me who coddle their plants with conversation, this is a comfort.

I think old Monsieur Vibert would approve.

CHAPTER 1

Artful Personalities

A GREAT ROSE—LIKE GREAT ART, MUSIC, AND literature—can stir the passions. Thus, it comes as no surprise that many hybridizers of the past found naming inspiration in the creative geniuses of their age. The ravishing blossoms that have survived—whether simple and refined or gloriously provocative—still have the power to arouse the poet in you, invite you to ponder nature, move you to sing.

OMAR KHAYYÁM
14

SOUVENIR DE VICTOR HUGO
16

RUBENS
18

MOZART
20

ANAÏS SÉGALAS
22

REDOUTÉ
24

EXCELLENZ VON SCHUBERT
28

GOETHE
30

FANTIN-LATOUR
32

MME. EUGÈNE E. MARLITT
34

Omar Khayyám

TYPE: DAMASK • INTRODUCED: 1893

PARENTAGE: UNKNOWN

Dig a little further than the familiar line "A jug of wine, a loaf of bread—and thou" in *The Rubáiyát of Omar Khayyám,* and you'll soon find yourself in a reverie of wild roses. So how could there *not* be a rose honoring the Islamic sage who wrote of them?

Omar Khayyám—aka Ghiyath al-Din Abu al-Fath 'Umar ibn Ibrahim al-Nisaburi al-Khayyami—lived from about 1048 to 1122 in Persia. A tentmaker's son revered in his lifetime as a mathematician, astronomer, and philosopher, he wrote treatises on everything from Euclidean algebra and geometry to music theory and existentialist thought. The accuracy of his calculations astonishes scientists today; his revision of the Persian calendar, which occupied him for many years, is still used in Iran.

In the West, however, Omar Khayyám's fame springs from the poetry of his *Rubáiyát,* brought to light in 1859 by the British writer Edward Fitzgerald. In his nonliteral "rendering," as he called it, Fitzgerald concentrated on only about a hundred of the thousand or so *rubáiyát* (or four-line stanzas)—but their live-for-today hedonism was enough to intoxicate the era's literary types. Exclusive Omar Khayyám clubs for gentlemen sprang up in England, America, and Germany. A British Omarian collected seeds of the 'Omar Khayyám' rose at the sage's grave in Nashipur, Iran. In 1893, he and other club members planted a bush ceremoniously at the foot of Fitzgerald's grave in Suffolk, where it still grows.

In spite of the rose's heady Damask fragrance, the American Rose Society considers 'Omar Khayyám' a mere curiosity due to its gawky nature. But perhaps, as Omar might say, this attitude too shall pass. Romantic gardeners find the loose, quartered blossoms, as free-spirited as a hedonist's temperament, perfectly fitting: They look tipsy, as if they've had a little too much to drink.

Souvenir de Victor Hugo

TYPE: TEA • INTRODUCED: 1885

PARENTAGE: 'COMTESSE DE LABARATHE' X 'REGULUS'

When Victor-Marie Hugo, the powerhouse of French literature, died in 1885 at the age of eighty-three, more than two million people followed his coffin to his burial place at the Panthéon in Paris. A profusion of roses bearing Victor Hugo's name followed, including a dark red Hybrid Perpetual by Joseph Schwartz, a bright pink Hybrid Perpetual by Jean Pernet, and this apricot blend Tea by Joseph Bonnaire—the antique namesake you're most likely to find today. Bonnaire may have felt closer to Hugo than the others; he lived part of his life, during Hugo's era, in Paris.

Hugo had even more personalities than his namesake roses. A lightning rod for social change, he fled France after Napoléon III seized power in 1851. During nineteen years in exile with his family, mostly on the remote island of Guernsey in the English Channel off the coast of Normandy, he railed at the emperor from afar, spewing out antigovernment pamphlets that were smuggled into France and diligently confiscated.

If Napoléon I was the nineteenth century's heart, Hugo became its conscience after writing his 1862 masterpiece *Les Misérables* about unjust penal laws, mistreatment of the poor, and the July Revolution of 1830. Although *The Hunchback of Notre-Dame,* first published in 1831, had made Hugo internationally famous, *Les Misérables* made him—at least in the minds of his countrymen—immortal.

With a Catholic mother active in the royalist underground and a brutish military father who lived with another woman, Hugo became a man of contradictions: wealthy by his thirties, but miserly; a strong father to his four children, but a notorious philanderer. Although Hugo never left his wife, Adèle, his family had a constant shadow in Juliette Drouet, his soul mate for more than fifty years.

Somehow, he also found time to draw illustrations and write seven novels, poetry, essays, and political propaganda. The success of *Les Contemplations,* a famous volume of poetry, enabled Hugo to buy Hauteville House, his home in Guernsey. His transcendent writing revolutionized the French language, appealing to the masses even when establishment critics derided it. Except for the two family members who landed in insane asylums, the whole Hugo clan served as his personal librarians, secretaries, and copyists.

Hugo, who obsessively drew the letters *V* and *H* across his work, viewed the universe with an omnipotent eye, often reshaping reality to suit his vision. The poet Jean Cocteau wittily suggested, "Victor Hugo was a madman who thought he was Victor Hugo." On the other hand, biographer Graham Robb calls Hugo's work "the most lucid case of madness in literature."

As colorfully intense as the literary paragon's personality, Bonnaire's 'Souvenir de Victor Hugo' puts out its vibrantly shaded blooms on burgundy-hued new growth. Its scent, too, is robust—you might even say dominating. The heavy flowers nod on their stems as if weighed by deep thoughts, constantly churning.

One doesn't have to gaze long at the tawny tones of 'Rubens' to see in it the luminous skin of the goddesses who frolic in *The Feast of Venus, The Three Graces,* and *The Judgment of Paris.* The Flemish Baroque painter Peter Paul Rubens (1577–1640) knew this flesh intimately, having modeled it after that of his young second wife.

Rubens spent the first part of his career in Italy, soaking up lessons from Renaissance masterpieces. Returning home to the Netherlands, he became the most famous artist of his time. His paintings have an unmistakable energy—some are so full of fury, you can almost hear the subjects screaming and the swords clanging.

Although Europe's royal families sparred over religious differences, many of them received the likable Rubens as an honored guest and occasional diplomat at their courts: the Infanta Isabella and Archduke Albert of the Spanish Netherlands, England's King Charles I, Spain's King Philip IV, and France's Marie de Médicis all patronized him. At the artist's lavish compound in Antwerp, assistants helped churn out portraits, altarpieces, massive allegorical "cycles," even tapestry designs and bookplates.

Given his friendships, Rubens could have married into the nobility after his first wife, Isabella Brandt, died during a plague. Instead, he pragmatically chose Isabella's niece Helena Fourment, a wealthy merchant's daughter. He told a friend he preferred a wife who wouldn't blush when he picked up his paintbrushes. Helena, exceeding that modest expectation, became his late-career muse. Often depicted with her ample breasts, well-cushioned hips, and bunion-covered toes exposed, she appears in everything from quiet paintings such as *The Allegory of Peace* to turbulent, epic-scale works such as *The Massacre of the Innocents* and *The Horrors of War.*

As a testament to Rubens's lasting influence, several French hybridizers dedicated roses to him centuries after his death. Jean Laffay's amaranth-colored Hybrid Perpetual first appeared in 1852, twelve years before Victor Verdier's "pansy-colored" Hybrid Perpetual and more than a hundred years before the Guajard family's red Hybrid Tea, 'Rubens'. However, for those who appreciate fleshy glory, there's no better 'Rubens' than the circa 1859 Tea rose shown here. Little is known about its creators, a prolific company listed in nineteenth-century rose catalogs only as Moreau-Robert. But they clearly understood Rubens's earthly passions.

In its sensuous form and color, 'Rubens' celebrates—as the master himself did—Helena's voluptuous spirit. With a heady fragrance like well-steeped tea, it's a rose that invites you, charmingly, into its dewy bosom.

Rubens

TYPE: TEA • INTRODUCED: 1859

PARENTAGE: UNKNOWN

Mozart

TYPE: HYBRID MUSK • INTRODUCED: 1937

PARENTAGE: 'ROBIN HOOD' X 'ROTE PHARISÄER'

His sublime compositions may be classical, but Wolfgang Amadeus Mozart (1756–1791) was a pop star for the ages. No other composer has been so intriguingly fictionalized onstage and in film.

Peter Lambert, the father of the German rose industry, didn't have to fantasize, however, when he created his 'Mozart'. Awash with clusters of pure, simple blooms, the rose aptly reflects the clarity and delicacy of its namesake's music.

Mozart, a precocious child prodigy, toured the courts of Europe with his musical family until striking out, rather recklessly, on his own in his teens. Sensing that his time was too valuable to be spent writing court dances, the demure genius shunned the patronage of nobles. At the same time, he couldn't afford to look like a starving artist, so he and his wife, Constanze, lived lavishly, often in debt. They rented large apartments, and Mozart once bought a carriage just so they could arrive in style at a premiere.

Mozart's breakthrough hit, the first opera written for a paying public, came in 1791 with *The Magic Flute,* sung in lowbrow German and riddled with references to the then-subversive culture of the Freemasons. The opera's success enabled Mozart's producer to build his own theater. Unfortunately, the composer didn't enjoy his big moment for long; he died at thirty-five, three months after the premiere. Although Constanze insisted her husband was poisoned, music historians point to a litany of illnesses that caught up with the always frail genius.

Mozart's legacy includes more than twenty works for the stage, among them the operas *The Marriage of Figaro* and *Don Giovanni,* as well as symphonies, chamber music, piano concertos, and choral works, such as the remarkable but unfinished *Requiem.* Emotionally potent and complex, much of his music was compositionally ahead of its time. (Emperor Joseph II complained that it had too many notes.)

With his roses, sometimes called Lambertianas, Lambert showed a connoisseur's understanding of the great composer's ear. Clusters of small flowers float on 'Mozart' like the intricate allegro runs of a divertimento score. Their sunny stamens perch sublimely like high notes above the petals, which fade from a perky pink to soft white as they mature—a visual symphony, to be sure.

Anaïs Ségalas

TYPE: CENTIFOLIA • INTRODUCED: 1837

PARENTAGE: A GALLICA X A CENTIFOLIA

The great French rose hybridizer Jean-Pierre Vibert introduced 'Anaïs Ségalas' around the same time the woman it honors created a stir with her poetry collection *Les Oiseaux de passage* (Migratory Birds). It's possible that the poet's husband purchased the rose for her as a celebratory gift. Vibert may have read Théophile Gautier's reviews of Ségalas's work in *Le Figaro* and may even have met her. It isn't likely, however, that he read her poetry or exotic fiction, a nineteenth-century genre aimed at female audiences.

While more firebrandish feminists fought in revolutionary skirmishes, Ségalas (1814–1893) stayed true to her petit-bourgeois roots. "God save me from such revolutionary ideas; I am not one of those women who have turned their shawl into a flag," she huffed in her 1847 collection *La Femme* (Woman). Today's feminist ideals would have offended her, too. Witness this line from 1844's *Enfantines* (The Childish Ones): "Love, pray, dream, that's the existence of all women."

The daughter of a Picard Frenchman and a white Creole from Haiti, Anaïs Ménard married Victor Ségalas, a royal court lawyer, when she was fifteen. Within a year, the dramatic beauty with expressive eyes and dark hair had published her first collection of poems, *Les Algériennes* (The Algerians), exploring the issue of slavery in France's colonies. Her views apparently evolved over the years, as political fashion dictated; a more prejudiced attitude prevailed in her much-reprinted 1885 novel *Récits des Antilles: Le Bois de la Soufrière* (Tales from the Antilles: The Wood of Soufrière). Mid-career, Ségalas contributed to *Le Journal des Femmes,* wrote criticism, helped organize learning centers for women, and penned a comedy for Paris's famed Odéon theater.

Gardens comprised an essential part of Ségalas's universe. Reveling in nature's cycles in the poem "Bertile," she contemplates a blooming rose the day after giving birth to a daughter—"another celestial pink." The shifting pink hues of 'Anaïs Ségalas' might inspire you to poetic thoughts, too. In the rose's profusion of petals, a sense of bourgeois opulence prevails. Note the contrast between the soft, silvery pinks along the flowers' edges and their intensely colored centers: This rose, like its namesake, is mindful of outward appearances.

While political upheaval swirled around him in the late eighteenth and early nineteenth centuries, history's favorite botanical illustrator kept busy with his paintbrushes—pleasing everyone from royalists to republicans without losing his head.

Born in what is now Belgium, Pierre-Joseph Redouté (1759–1840) came from a family of artists. After learning to draw as a young boy, he moved to Paris in his early twenties, hoping to build on the tradition of master floral painters such as Jan Brueghel the Elder and Jan van Huysum.

With intrepid plant explorers of the period bringing home botanical discoveries by the shipload and wealthy enthusiasts anxious to document them, Redouté's timing was impeccable. He learned to paint with watercolors on vellum at the Jardin du Roi (Garden of the King) in Paris, then improved on the art form by employing the Italian stippling technique that gives his illustrations such brilliant precision. Patronized by the amateur botanist Charles-Louis L'Héritier de Brutelle (who, years later, was brutally murdered), Redouté also spent a year in London studying plants at Kew Gardens and meeting the plant world glitterati. When he returned to France, Queen Marie Antoinette made him her official court artist and teacher.

It's hard to believe the French Academy bothered with a Salon the year the queen was guillotined, but they did, and the untouchable Redouté showed his work for the first time. He made a living documenting the country's national gardens during the Revolution; then, not too many years later, he sailed to Egypt as part of Napoléon Bonaparte's team of naturalists. (He famously remarked to the ambitious general, "Painting flowers may be something small, but it is what I do best, because it is what I love most.")

Commissions from Napoléon's flower-loving wife, Joséphine, soon put Redouté on the map in a more profitable way. Working with the botanist Etienne Pierre Ventenat, he produced *Jardin de la Malmaison, Les Liliacées,* and, finally, *Les Roses* for the empress. Joséphine—whose aim was to own every rose variety in creation—didn't live to see *Les Roses* finished. When Napoléon's reign ended, Redouté went to work for the next regime at the National Museum of Natural History. He served one more king, Louis-Philippe, before dying at eighty while painting a lily.

David Austin, the eminent British hybridizer, believes Redouté was the best rose painter ever. "It seemed only right that there should be a rose bearing his name," Austin says. 'Redouté' is typically light pink, but sports (naturally occuring hybrids) that revert to its ivory-colored parent, 'Mary Rose', can occur. In an artistic mood, one might imagine the lushly formed rosettes of 'Redouté' as layer upon layer of vellum sheets awaiting the master's hand. They would be scented papers, mind you. Evoking the past deliciously, their strong, honey-almond fragrance can fill a room.

Redouté

TYPE: SHRUB • INTRODUCED: 1992

PARENTAGE: SPORT OF 'MARY ROSE'

Excellenz von Schubert

TYPE: HYBRID MUSK • INTRODUCED: 1909

PARENTAGE: 'MADAME NORBERT LEVAVASSEUR' X 'FRAU KARL DRUSCHKI'

Franz Peter Schubert's bouncy piano quintet the *Trout* may be instantly recognizable, but his forte was the lied, a plaintive song form known for its pastoral images of lonely wanderers. Schubert wrote more than six hundred lieder, often adapted from the poetry of Johann Wolfgang von Goethe, Friedrich von Schiller, Wilhelm Müller, and other German Romantics. "When I wished to sing of love, it turned to sorrow," wrote Schubert, who lived from 1797 to 1828.

Born into a humble Viennese family, Schubert lost his mother when he was fifteen. His father, a respected schoolmaster, taught Franz to play the violin but expected all of his sons to become teachers. He wasn't pleased when Franz, on scholarship at an imperial school, quit to devote himself to music.

Although it's possible that rose breeder Peter Lambert had one of his German customers in mind when he named 'Excellenz von Schubert'—as the composer's name doesn't include the designation "von"—the abundant sprays of small, pom-pom-like blossoms on the rose are a lovely reminder of Schubert's prolific output. During his phenomenal eighteenth year alone, Schubert composed about 150 lieder, as well as 2 symphonies, 4 operas, and 2 masses, among other works. Historians believe he was inspired at the time by an angelic-voiced singer and baker's daughter, Therese Grob, whom he loved but couldn't marry because she belonged to higher society.

Not that Schubert moped for long. Lovably pudgy, bespectacled, and high-spirited, he wrote music during the day and hung out at night with his bookish buddies—the first Bohemians—in the coffeehouses and taverns of Vienna. Middle-class friends and noble patrons often housed Schubert and supplied him with paper. (No trifling expense, as he wrote voraciously.) At parties known as "Schubertiads," his friends actively promoted his music.

It's a shame that no one knows who created 'Fantin-Latour', because he would be celebrated for it. Experts aren't even sure quite where to place 'Fantin-Latour' among the rose classes. Given its nodding "cabbage rose" form—a favorite of painters since the seventeenth century—it is most often grouped with the Centifolias.

French artist Ignace Henri Jean Théodore Fantin-Latour (1836–1904) loved to depict roses. Fantin-Latour and his wife, Victoria—who also specialized in still lifes— spent their summers in Normandy, where they grew many kinds of flowers. Arranging blooms loosely in simple glass vases, Fantin-Latour captured their varied forms with modernistic brushwork and a strikingly objective eye.

Fantin-Latour's influential English dealers, Edwin and Ruth Edwards, sold most of his more than eight hundred still lifes to fashionable Londoners. At home, the artist was known as an academic who created "serious" art for the Salon, Paris's official annual competition. His group portraits of his contemporaries—especially *L'Atelier des Batignolles* (1870) and *The Corner of the Table* (1872)—have a candid quality, as if he'd caught his intellectual friends chatting, smoking, and drinking together after dinner. Although stylistically more conservative than his Impressionist friends, including Edgar Degas, Edouard Manet, and Claude Monet, Fantin-Latour experimented briefly with edgier techniques: His *La Féerie* hung in the notorious "alternative" 1863 Salon de Refusés, which officially launched the Impressionist movement.

Self-portraits show Fantin-Latour growing moodier with age. Art historians say the era's wars made him paranoid and that he'd cross the street if he saw a soldier coming his way. Fantasy provided at least a temporary escape late in his life, when Fantin-Latour made lithographs based on the music and operas of Romantic composers. Some of these works strongly influenced the next generation's Symbolist movement.

Since the provenance of the rose 'Fantin-Latour' is a mystery, who knows whether its namesake ever planted or painted it? He probably would have loved its luminous color and sublime shape. With a bush of vivid green leaves and nearly smooth canes, 'Fantin-Latour' brings a picture-perfect palette to the garden.

No matter that she wrote florid prose. The German romance novelist E. Marlitt churned out trans-Atlantic best sellers in the late nineteenth and early twentieth centuries. In a twist her readers would have appreciated, her namesake rose appears in the guise of multiple identities—also the kind of conundrum Antique Rose aficionados love to ponder.

In the late 1980s, Texas horticulturalist William Welch discovered a charming and exceptionally fragrant mystery rose growing in the Louisiana garden of his wife's grandmother. As is customary with unidentified Antiques, Welch named the rose 'Maggie', after its owner. Some experts now believe 'Maggie' is the same rose American nurseries sold in the early 1900s variously as 'Eugenie Marlitt' and 'Mme. Eugène E. Marlitt'. This rose's creator, the pioneering European breeder Rudolf Geschwind, called the rose 'Julius Fabianics de Misefa'—a name that may have been deemed too complicated to sell well on this side of the Atlantic. (This is a very well-traveled rose: Indian rosarians, who grow it for garlands, know it as 'Kakinada Red'.)

And the plot thickens. There was no Mme. Eugène or Eugenie Marlitt. These variants represent one Eugenie John (1825–1887), a German writer who, given the social strictures of her era, concealed her feminine identity with the nom de plume E. Marlitt.

Born to a well-off merchant's family in the ancient city of Arnstadt, hometown of Johann Sebastian Bach, Eugenie might not have become a writer if she hadn't gone deaf. Trained as an opera singer and patronized by Princess Mathilde von Schwarzburg-Sonderhausen, the future writer performed for almost a decade in the great halls of Vienna and Leipzig. When she lost her hearing, she joined court society as the princess's companion. About ten years later, using her nom de plume, she began writing serials for a German magazine. The success of her stories and novels gave her the financial independence to buy her own villa, Marlittshouse. She wrote thirteen books that were translated for her American and English fans with such enticing titles as *The Old Mam'selle's Secret* and *The Second Wife*.

The author didn't get to enjoy Geschwind's rose, since it was introduced after her death. But the rose and its German namesake do appear to be two of a kind. Her face framed by brunette ringlets, the handsome Eugenie had a razor-sharp expression. The blooms of 'Mme. Eugène E. Marlitt' are somewhat tightly coiled, too. And as for their intense color and spicy fragrance, no delicate, powdery pink would do to commemorate the author of *The Lady with the Rubies*.

Mme. Eugène E. Marlitt

TYPE: BOURBON • INTRODUCED: 1900

PARENTAGE: UNKNOWN

CHAPTER 2

Heroes
&
Heroines

BECAUSE THE ROSE INDUSTRY TOOK ROOT IN France during the nineteenth century, when revolution and upheaval reigned, a thorny army of genteel generals and other French heroes march onward through gardens today. The twentieth century brought new displays of valor, with roses named for preservationists whose weapons were more likely to be shovels than swords. Without their influence, many of the marvelous, old-fashioned cultivars we enjoy today might be lost.

NAPOLÉON
38

JEANNE D'ARC
40

JACQUES CARTIER
42

CARDINAL DE RICHELIEU
44

ARCHDUKE CHARLES
46

CONSTANCE SPRY
50

LAMARQUE
52

HENRI MARTIN
54

CAPTAIN THOMAS
56

ROBIN HOOD
60

Napoléon

TYPE: C. • INTRODUCED: C. 1835

PARENTAGE: UNKNOWN

Military genius. Ruthless despot. Charismatic commander. Shrewd propagandist. Napoléon Bonaparte (1769–1821) was all of the above. Although he ruled France for less than fifteen years, the "Napoleonic era" lasted almost a century.

Born on the island of Corsica to Italian parents, Napoléon was leading the French army by the age of twenty-six. An ambitious military hero, he had all the right qualities to take control in an unstable revolutionary environment—including a large ego. At thirty, he staged a coup and gave himself the title of First Consul, a powerful position as the leader of a three-member Consulate that ran France; five years later, he crowned himself Emperor of France.

At the pinnacle of his reign—1805 and 1806—as his armies decimated Austrian troops at Ulm, Russian troops at Austerlitz, and the Prussians at Jena and Auerstadt, Napoléon seemed invincible. In Paris, a "new money" culture of Empire high style and voguish neoclassicism reigned, driven by Napoléon's interest in antiquities from lands he'd conquered. An adept administrator, he established the Bank of France and important legal codes, streamlined the tax system, and built a much-needed freshwater system in Paris. But Napoléon's empire wasn't all rosy. French newspapers nearly disappeared under his harsh censorship, their numbers shrinking from about one thousand in 1799 to four "authorized" publications in 1811. Women lost the right to own property.

And the emperor quickly self-destructed, growing so irrational that he failed to adapt as the scale of warfare grew. His disastrous march into Russia in 1812 reduced his troops to a bedraggled bunch. In 1814, as his allied enemies marched down Paris's Champs-Elysées, Napoléon fled to Elba. He left behind not only his beloved Empress Joséphine, whom he'd divorced in order to sire an heir, but his young second wife, Archduchess Marie-Louise of Austria, and his son, Napoléon II.

Napoléon's surprise return in 1815, known as the Hundred Days, ended at Waterloo, where the British and the Prussians finished off the remnants of his once fierce Imperial Guard. The former emperor spent his last six years on the remote island of Saint Helena, writing his memoirs. In a show of patriotism, King Louis-Philippe had Napoléon's body exhumed in 1840 and reburied at Paris's Les Invalides.

When Napoléon was in the field, the Duke of Wellington once said, "He made the difference of forty thousand men." Napoléon's namesake rose is rather modest, considering his epic personality. Perhaps the French hybridizer Jean Laffay was simply trying to bring him down to size? Curiously, the rose is also sold as 'Madness of Corsica'. And its China-type heritage suggests the dictator's later Napoleonic qualities: Its petals grow more pointed, darker, and disheveled as they age.

The history of France might have run a different course if the farmer's daughter known as La Pucelle (the Maiden) hadn't charged into the Hundred Years' War in 1429. For more than six hundred years, her fascinating story has intrigued writers, dramatists, musicians, and painters. Some, however, take substantial liberties with reality; Shakespeare cast her as a villain in *Henry VI*.

Jean-Pierre Vibert's Alba rose 'Jeanne d'Arc' represents her saintly character more accurately. A commanding presence in the garden, with milky, slightly blushing blossoms, the rose seems as pure and forthright as the young woman who demanded an army from her country's dauphin in order to save his crown.

Born in the Champagne village of Domrémy, Joan of Arc (1412–1431) was a pious child who convinced the authorities, at age seventeen, that she should be given armor, horses, and leadership of the French army. In truth, the dauphin Charles needed a miracle. British forts surrounded the walled city of Orléans, France's last nationalist stronghold. Joan's reinforcements reenergized the troops, and she won over skeptical commanders with her battle strategies and courage. Although she took an arrow through the shoulder, the siege ended nine days after her arrival.

As much a spiritual force as a warrior, Joan carried a flowing white standard into battle to rally her men. She wielded a legendary sword primarily for chastising troops—forbidding pillaging and debauchery and chasing prostitutes from her camps. And she exuded goodness, wearing elaborately laced pants and armor to protect her virginity.

Even after Charles was crowned king, his French rivals, the Burgundians, remained British allies. Favoring compromise, Charles cut his war budget and severely curtailed La Pucelle's actions. She had only a few troops at her side in 1430, when the Burgundians ambushed her at Compiègne and sold her to the British. A captive at Rouen for a year, Joan held her own through a sensational trial run largely by French judges. After her jailers took her dress, leaving her only pants to wear, the court finally convicted her of heresy on the slim charge of cross-dressing. They burned nineteen-year-old Joan alive, as onlookers wept. Many years later, her conviction was overturned; she became Saint Joan of Arc in 1920.

Legend has it that Joan was driven by divine voices. 'Jeanne d'Arc' is heaven-sent, too. In early summer, when its blossoms float across the plant's tall, arching canes, you might imagine the undulating waves of our heroine's white battle flag in action. The finely serrated edges of its stunning blue-gray leaves hint at Joan's nonconformist nature, while its powdery scent implies an everlasting innocence.

Jeanne d'Arc

TYPE: ALBA • INTRODUCED: 1818

PARENTAGE: SEEDLING OF 'ELISA'

Jacques Cartier

TYPE: HYBRID PERPETUAL • INTRODUCED: 1868

PARENTAGE: UNKNOWN

Like other European explorers who crossed the Atlantic looking for a quick route to the Far East, Jacques Cartier (1491–1557) saw his hopes dashed. But North Americans—Canadians, especially—can thank him for naming the Lachine Rapids (which he thought would lead to China), Cap Diamant (whose quartz stone he mistook for diamonds), and Montreal.

Cartier was born into a family of mariners in Brittany. He didn't record his early voyages, although his Canadian journals suggest he was familiar with Brazil. Crossing the Atlantic in only twenty days in 1534, he explored the coast between Newfoundland and Quebec with a crew of sixty men and two ships. Depressed by the brutal spring weather and craggy landscape, he declared it "the land God allotted to Cain." Then came a blissful summer, discovery of the Eden-like edges of Prince Edward Island, and friendship with a large tribe of Iroquois. In place of riches, Cartier took home temporary captives—Iroquois chief Donnacona's two sons.

A year later, the chief's sons returned with Cartier to the Saint Lawrence River. This time, Cartier made his way to the peak he called Mont-Royal (now Montreal). In the abundant, wildlife-rich landscape of that autumn, Cartier found "as goodly a country as possibly with eye can be seen." He reported seeing all kinds of fantastical animals, including "fishes shaped like horses" (walruses) and white whales "headed like greyhounds." But back near Quebec, winter brought a scurvy attack that nearly killed all of Cartier's men. When native warriors threatened the following spring, it seemed prudent to leave. But Cartier again took home human bounty, including Chief Donnacona himself, who died in France.

Returning to Canada in 1541 to help establish a permanent French settlement, Cartier didn't fare as well. He arrived months ahead of the settlers, struggled through winter, and slipped back to France without permission, retiring comfortably to his hometown of Saint-Malo.

'Jacques Cartier', the rose, has caused almost as much confusion today as its namesake's exploration did in the sixteenth century. Although the French firm of Moreau-Robert introduced it in 1868, a shorter but otherwise identical rose by Jean Desprez, also a Frenchman, predates 'Jacques Cartier' by twenty-six years.

Desprez called his rose 'Marchesa Boccella'. Little is known about its namesake, although she was most likely married to the nineteenth-century Tuscan nobleman Cesare Boccella. A minor poet and friend of the composer Franz Liszt, Cesare Boccella translated several of Aleksandr Pushkin's works into Italian.

'Jacques Cartier' may soon fade into obscurity. The American Rose Society has ruled that the rose may be exhibited now only as 'Marchesa Boccella'. While there's a bit of the confused explorer in its scraggly petals, the rose's delicate nature and sweet scent beg to be identified with someone more demure and cultured.

Cardinal de Richelieu

TYPE: HYBRID CHINA • INTRODUCED: 1840

PARENTAGE: UNKNOWN

I f you give me six lines written by the most honest man, I will find something in them to hang him." So said a man one would not want to cross: King Louis XIII's cunning prime minister, Armand-Jean du Plessis, the cardinal of Richelieu (1585–1642).

Alexandre Dumas portrayed him as a ruthless villain in *The Three Musketeers*. The real cardinal, believing his king had divine right, destroyed the castles of nobles who had their own armies, weakened the Holy Roman Empire, and crushed Huguenot rebellions in the name of building an "absolute" monarchy. And yet, the man nicknamed the Red Eminence—for the huge red cape he often wore—also founded the French Academy, helped establish colonies, supported the arts, and appreciated gardens.

Befitting his complex character, the rose 'Cardinal de Richelieu' is an extraordinary specimen whose purple blooms bring authority and shock value to the garden. A Dutchman named Van Sian bred it and sold it, unnamed, to one of France's most prolific and prosperous early hybridizers, Jean Laffay. This was a "mid-career" rose for Laffay, who nurtured as many as two hundred thousand seedlings in his nursery. Why did it remind him of an infamous historical figure who'd died almost two hundred years earlier?

It's feasible that Laffay saw Philippe de Champaigne's notorious portrait of the cardinal hanging in a museum. During the cardinal's lifetime, the painting defied protocol by depicting the aristocratic official standing up—a pose that was ordinarily reserved for kings.

Regardless of Laffay's inspiration, we can't ignore the intriguing buds of the rose 'Cardinal de Richelieu'. Its plump shape perfectly mimics our hero's miter (or cap). As its blooms mature, an even fuller portrait emerges.

Peering into a blossom, one might imagine the cardinal's visage as it appears in Champaigne's portrait: In each button-eye center, his smallish face. In the faded inner petals, his white ecclesiastical collar. In the muddled mass all around, the drapery-like folds of his voluminous robe. The rose even smells right: It's a pinch peppery.

Only a warmonger would plant 'Archduke Charles' next to a rose named for anyone from Napoléon's camp, although it might discourage a *"coup de jardin."* The nobleman Erzherzog Karl von Österreich-Teschen (1771–1847) was one of Napoléon's most able and valiant opponents.

A nephew of Marie Antoinette's and brother of the Austrian emperor Francis II, the young archduke was proclaimed "the Savior of Germany" in 1796 after he drove French armies back across the Rhine. In 1809, he inflicted one of Napoléon's first major defeats at the Battle of Aspern-Essling. Although he lost the decisive Battle of Wagram—forcing Austria to cede Vienna temporarily to the French—the archduke proved to be more than a thorn in Napoléon's side. His tenacity and tactical skill cost the French army more than thirty thousand of its men.

The progressive archduke, who didn't agree with his brother's conservative policies, then retired to a life more befitting his station. He was, after all, a Hapsburg. Fortune treated him gently after he married Princess Henrietta of Nassau-Weilburg in 1815. Except for a son who died a few weeks after being born, their seven children lived long and married well. The archduke himself lived to be seventy-six—ancient in his era. Humbler than his nemesis, Napoléon, Charles didn't want a statue erected in his honor. His fans erected an equestrian monument to him anyway at Vienna's historic Heldenplatz after he died.

The archduke apparently didn't mind being honored with a rose, however. Feasibly, he could have visited Monsieur Jean Laffay's huge nursery near Paris and selected his namesake from the thousands of roses Laffay grew, or perhaps 'Archduke Charles' was presented to him as a gift. The rose's fruity scent is mild-mannered, like the archduke himself. Although many roses have blossoms that fade in color as they mature, the flowers of 'Archduke Charles' dramatically deepen from light pink to crimson—perfectly suited to a royal whose richest moments came later in life.

Archduke Charles

TYPE: CHINA • INTRODUCED: PRIOR TO 1837

PARENTAGE: RELATED TO 'PARSON'S PINK CHINA'

Constance Spry

TYPE: SHRUB • INTRODUCED: 1961

PARENTAGE: 'BELLE ISIS' X 'DAINTY MAID'

Years before the world loved Martha Stewart, the iconic Constance Spry (1886–1960) kept all of Britain well decorated. The world's first celebrity floral designer, she lived by the mantra "Flowers are for everyone."

"There were no half-measures with Mrs. Spry," wrote her good friend, the legendary rosarian Graham Stuart Thomas. He knew a full-measure rose when he saw it, too. This lush specimen was brought to him unnamed in 1960—a few months after Constance died—by David Austin, a then-unknown farmer just beginning to produce Modern Roses with an "Old Rose" soul. In what Austin calls "a great piece of beginner's luck," 'Constance Spry' was a hit, launching an English rose craze that's still going strong.

Born Constance Fletcher, the woman who inspired the rose didn't hit her stride so smoothly. Initially working as a community health instructor, she left her first husband during World War I and moved with her young son to London. There, she became the popular headmistress at one of England's first mandatory schools for teenage factory workers—a place in dreary East London she was determined to make an "oasis of elegance." She kept the halls decorated resourcefully with plants from her garden—including unexpected but common hedgerow plants, twigs, and leaves—which she frequently displayed in such novel containers as shells, birdcages, and soup tureens scavenged from junk shops.

A fortuitous gig designing window displays for a hip new Mayfair perfume store, Atkinson's on Bond Street, changed Constance's life. At age forty, she leaped from social worker to high-society darling. (She also found happiness at home, finally marrying Shav Spry, a cultured, world-wise accountant with whom she'd exchanged love letters, long distance, for years.) Soon, Constance's busy shop had seventy employees and an upscale clientele that included the royal family. The duke of Windsor and Wallis Simpson brought her to France to create the decorations for their wedding. Her crowning achievement, some years later, was her floral décor for the coronation of Queen Elizabeth II.

In the 1940s, Constance had England's largest collection of Antique Roses. They survived World War II, but she wanted insurance in case they didn't survive a move to a new home. She first called Graham Thomas, who was then a nursery manager, shortly after the war to see if he'd make cuttings from her plants. She'd amassed "the most sumptuous varieties," he wrote, and "the long French names flowed from her." Before showing Thomas her garden, Constance drew him inside her home, where she'd set a pale green satin tablecloth with a voluptuous assortment of purple and maroon Moss roses, Gallicas, and Centifolias. Smitten by the sight, he agreed to take on the project.

Ever the teacher, Constance parlayed her success into a school for domestic sciences and a dozen books. Constance Spry Ltd. is still operating, and you can still read our heroine's books. But to remember her as her friends did—a lively little woman bearing armloads of fragrant sprays—seek out 'Constance Spry' in early summer, when her pink blooms cascade fragrantly over trellises with the "glorious blowsiness" she was known for, unforgettably fragrant.

Lamarque

TYPE: NOISETTE • INTRODUCED: 1830

PARENTAGE: 'BLUSH NOISETTE' X 'PARK'S YELLOW TEA-SCENTED CHINA'

orn in Saint-Sever, a town in southwest France, Jean Maximilien Lamarque (1770–1832) was a thinking man's warrior—well educated, humane, even poetic. "He was as eloquent as he had been valiant; a sword was discernible in his speech," wrote Victor Hugo.

Dramatically fictionalizing Lamarque's funeral in his masterpiece *Les Misérables,* Hugo made this Napoleonic general even larger than he was in life. Hugo imagined that the death of the popular Lamarque sparked the antimonarchist riots that rocked Paris in June 1832.

At the very least, it inspired the naming of a rose. No doubt the gentleman who created 'Lamarque'—an amateur rose breeder known today only as Monsieur Maréchal—was among the general's fans. Maréchal, a gardener at La Croix Montaille château in Angers, is said to have raised the seedling in a window box. He initially called the rose after himself, most likely changing it to the highly marketable 'Lamarque' after the general's death.

Lamarque wasn't at Waterloo in 1815, much to his dismay. But he kept the battle alive in his heart, as Hugo suggested, "majestically preserving" its sadness and "paying hardly any attention to intervening events." That's a slight exaggeration: Lamarque was a passionate advocate for the rights of farmers and a liberal opponent of the Restoration government. (One might keep this in mind when placing 'Lamarque' in the garden: His preferred position would be between the left and the extreme left.) But he never stopped believing in Napoléon. According to legend, as Lamarque lay dying of cholera, he uttered the word "fatherland" with his last breath.

After Napoléon's defeat, Lamarque spent three years exiled in Belgium and Holland. Here, his enlightened side emerged: He translated James McPherson's Ossian poetry cycle, taken from an ancient Celtic epic that also fascinated Sir Walter Scott and Johann Wolfgang von Goethe.

In a portrait made during his prime, the general looks more the romantic than the warrior. He's slightly preoccupied, gazing through his heavy-lidded eyes and across his prominent Gallic nose at something far-off. 'Lamarque', likewise, is a dreamy rose. Its shapely flowers call to mind the general's full lips and wavy hair. Its lemon-tinted center reflects his heart of gold, and its heady Tea fragrance could send anyone into an Ossian swoon. Appropriately, it's a Climber: General Lamarque's most audacious victory came when he scaled the highest cliffs of Capri for a surprise attack on the British.

Henri Martin

TYPE: MOSS • INTRODUCED: 1863

PARENTAGE: UNKNOWN X *CENTIFOLIA MUSCOSA*

So what if his magnum opus was a little suspect? Americans have good reason to love the French historian Bon-Louis-Henri Martin (1810–1883): He led the fundraising campaign to build the Statue of Liberty.

Some years earlier, Martin wrote *Histoire de France,* a nineteen-volume work published between 1838 and 1853. One of the first major chronicles of France's development, from its Celtic origins to the beginning of the French Revolution, the project won several major prizes from the French Academy and catapulted Martin into Paris's elite intellectual, academic, and political circles. Still, critics questioned Martin's spin. As one English reviewer commented, "He writes with the ardor of patriotic zeal, perhaps sometimes with the blindness of patriotic bigotry." A fellow professor politely called *Histoire de France* "more political and philosophical than literary."

Raised in Saint-Quentin, a city in northern France where national pride ran deep, Martin was pressured by his family to become a notary. At age twenty, he left for Paris with a poet friend and cowrote several historical romance novels, including the successful *Wolfthurm.*

With their government seesawing between emperors, kings, republics, and occasional foreign occupiers, Parisian intellectuals often discussed how society should function. Martin was among the Saint-Simonians, early socialists who argued for the importance of a strong working class. He also followed the eccentric religious philosophies of Jean Reynaud, who believed that after death, souls progress through the solar system.

Martin's biographer, Gabriel Hanotaux, calls him an austere and honest "man of Plutarch." Martin loved art, especially sculpture, but approached it with a practical eye. "A visit to the antiquities of the Louvre with him was a lesson in morals," Hanotaux wrote.

Martin and the young sculptor Frédéric-Auguste Bartholdi were among those gathered one night in 1865 at the home of the statesman and writer Edouard de Laboulaye when Laboulaye proposed the idea for the Statue of Liberty. The project took twenty-one years, delayed by the Franco-Prussian War and fund-raising issues. Martin mounted the French campaign to raise money for the sculpture, while Joseph Pulitzer led the American campaign to pay for the pedestal. Unfortunately, Martin died three years before the statue was delivered.

Perhaps if more people remembered his story, the rose 'Henri Martin' wouldn't also be known as 'Red Moss'. The great hybridizer Jean Laffay honored his countryman with the name long before the Statue of Liberty campaign. The rose is treasured today for its hairy—or mossy—buds. Although we'll never know if Laffay made the connection, the real Henri Martin looked a bit mossy, too. In an 1880 photograph, his face is perfectly framed by a mustache and muttonchops of pure white that glow against his ruddy skin.

One of the most dynamic rose hybridizers of the early twentieth century, Captain George C. Thomas Jr. (1873–1932) was a hero on several kinds of battlefields—from the front lines of World War I to the more prosaic combat zones of gardening, golf, and deep-sea fishing.

He endowed this simple but elegant rose with his own name, 'George C. Thomas Jr.'—a good indication that it was his favorite. Six years after he died, his daughter had it introduced to commerce under the more authoritative and memorable moniker 'Captain Thomas'.

The son of a prominent Philadelphia financier, Thomas discovered the world of roses when he was in his late twenties, just before he married the equally well-heeled sportswoman Ednah Ridge. Never one to consider his hobbies idle pastimes, Thomas also designed his first golf courses at this time and watched his English setters win Best of Breed at the Westminster Kennel Club show. (One wonders how he found time for a wife and family.)

Thomas acquired his military title in his forties, during World War I, when he enlisted as a pilot in the American Expeditionary Forces. Funding most of his unit's expenses, he led the first active American bombing squad in France, miraculously surviving three plane crashes.

After the war, Thomas moved his family to Beverly Hills for better rose-growing conditions. At their Rancho Ednada estate in California, he built one of the world's largest private gardens, with about fifteen hundred varieties of roses, an orchard of rare fruit trees, desert plants, and tropical specimens.

As prolific with a pen as he was with a spade, Thomas published two rose books, *The Practical Book of Outdoor Rose-Growing* in 1914 and *Roses for All American Climates* in 1924. He also penned the now-classic *Golf Architecture in America* in 1927 and *Game Fish of the Pacific* in 1930.

Thomas produced some of his best golf course designs in California, and traces of that work are still visible on a few holes at Los Angeles's Riviera Country Club. Unfortunately, that's more than we'll ever see of his magnificent garden. It disappeared after Thomas died at fifty-eight of a heart attack, and Rancho Ednada was subdivided. While Ednah kept the house, Californians still love to dish the (unproven) dirt that she leveled the captain's roses out of spite, because he'd named a rose for another woman.

Of all his accomplishments, Thomas was proudest of his roses. He introduced about forty varieties to commerce, including a series dedicated to his family's Pennsylvania estate with names such as 'Bloomfield Dainty' and 'Bloomfield Abundance'. But his namesake, 'Captain Thomas', is in a class of its own, a golden boy with a hint of the heroic, and larger than life.

Captain Thomas

TYPE: LARGE-FLOWERED CLIMBER • INTRODUCED: 1938

PARENTAGE: 'BLOOMFIELD COMPLETENESS' X 'ATTRACTION'

Robin Hood

TYPE: HYBRID MUSK • INTRODUCED: 1927

PARENTAGE: SEEDLING X 'EDITH CAVELL'

lthough his story is firmly fixed in the Middle Ages, Robin Hood's popularity has endured for more than six hundred years. Tales of the shrewd outlaw who steals from the rich and gives to the poor can be found everywhere from fifteenth-century ballads and poetry to contemporary films, comic books, and video games.

When the Reverend Joseph Pemberton developed his rose 'Robin Hood', the character was especially popular in children's literature. The plant's plentiful clusters of small, cheerful flowers suggest that the Reverend envisioned our hero in the midst of his band of Merry Men.

But did these lovable misfits ever exist outside the garden? Most scholars say no. Robin Hood was a common name during the Middle Ages, eventually becoming a generic alias for criminals. While the adventures of colorful thirteenth-century outlaws such as Fulk fitz Warin and Hereward may have fed the legend, scholars believe the "original" Robin Hood is a fictional composite.

Some of the familiar themes date back to *The Gest of Robyn Hode,* a long and influential ballad first published around 1500. This early Robin Hood is driven by his devotion to the Virgin Mary. Courteous toward women, he upholds high moral and social standards.

The action of *Gest* begins as sidekicks Little John, Will Scarlet, and Much deliver a dinner guest to Robin in the forest: an impoverished knight who owes a debt to an abbot. Robin gives the knight money. Later, he'll rob a monk who lies about how much money he's carrying. Other familiar themes appear, too: Little John ends up working for the sheriff in Nottingham, then robs him; the sheriff, lured into the woods, pardons Robin in exchange for his freedom; Robin and his men are baited by the authorities into an archery match but escape to the knight's castle; Robin kills the sheriff to save the knight; the king tricks Robin into serving him for a while; Robin and his men spend twenty-two more years in the forest; and finally, Robin is bled to death by his cousin, an evil prioress.

But elements of the legend have evolved continuously. The jovial Friar Tuck and Robin's love interest, Maid Marian, joined the folklore in the fifteenth century, when people often dressed as Robin Hood characters for May Day celebrations. The minstrel Allen a Dale came along in the seventeenth century, when Robin Hood ballads meant to be sung were printed for the masses on broadsides.

Robin Hood's character has also been adapted to suit shifting political climates: His religious zeal disappeared from the tales at about the time England broke from the Catholic Church. While he was a yeoman—a middle-class citizen—in the earliest ballads, in versions of the tale from later centuries, he acquired a noble title, the Earl of Huntington. And by the nineteenth century, he was more of a national hero than an anarchist, saving England from invading Normans. He's remained popular in part because he's human: He sometimes loses, and he gets roughed up.

An equally tough, vigorous, and healthy character, Reverend Pemberton's rose 'Robin Hood' was extremely popular in its early years and became a favorite parent plant for breeding programs. Unfortunately, Pemberton didn't get to see his creation become legendary; he died the year before the rose was introduced to commerce. 'Robin Hood' is as generous with its blossoms as its namesake was with honest travelers, offering up a near-constant supply of flowers.

CHAPTER 3

Nobles
&
Notables

ONE HARDLY HAS TO KNOW THAT SOME ROSES
honor courtly aristocrats of the past to sense a rich pedigree in their
opulent forms. And for good reason: Royals were hybridizers' first
patrons. Slowly, as a new breed of aristocrats usurped the ancien
regime, gardens filled with luscious 'Madames' and 'Sirs'—roses
honoring society swells and business tycoons whose magnificent
estates rivaled those of their imperial predecessors.

RENÉ D'ANJOU
64

LOUIS-PHILIPPE
66

ADÉLAÏDE D'ORLÉANS
68

KRONPRINZESSIN VIKTORIA VON PREUSSEN
72

DUCHESSE DE BRABANT
74

DUCHESSE DE GRAMONT
76

MME. ISAAC PEREIRE
78

MRS. PIERRE S. DU PONT
80

SIR THOMAS LIPTON
82

LADY WATERLOW
86

René d'Anjou

TYPE: MOSS • INTRODUCED: 1853

PARENTAGE: UNKNOWN

V isualize the mossy buds of 'René d'Anjou' as medieval knights' helmets, and you'll be in the right frame of mind to remember the fifteenth-century nobleman it honors.

Good King René, as he was fondly known, was a princely impresario fascinated by chivalry. He wrote the ultimate handbook on *pas d'armes, Treatise on the Form and Organization of a Tournament,* which celebrated knighthood as a friendly sport and jousting as court entertainment.

As a young man, René campaigned against the English with Joan of Arc. But he was better suited to faux warfare than the real thing. With his family's ties to royal houses in Spain and England as well as France, René had to uphold a laundry list of inherited titles in feudal battles. Rival princes captured him while he was defending the rights of his first wife, Isabel of Lorraine, after her father died. This landed him in a tower for several years. He was still there when his elder brother died and he inherited the rule of Naples, Jerusalem, and Aragon. Isabel went to Italy in his place, as queen. René eventually bought his way out of prison and joined her. But fighting was constant, and after four years, Alfonso V of Aragon evicted René and Isabel from Italy.

Strong women figured prominently in René's life. His mother, Yolande d'Aragon, helped raise France's King Charles VII (René's brother-in-law) and supported Joan of Arc. René and Isabel's second daughter, Marguerite, became infamous as the wife of Henry VI of England, a key agitator in the Wars of the Roses. After Isabel died in 1453, René married the much-younger Jeanne of Laval. He retired to a quiet life of reading and writing, producing poetry, satire, and the allegorical *Le Coeur d'amours espris,* which is often translated as *King René's Book of Love.*

The French nurseryman Monsieur Robert, whose first name isn't known, honored René centuries later with one of the first repeat-blooming Moss roses. Monsieur Robert lived in Angers, the town where René was born; he quite likely toured the king's Anjou fortress, which is still a landmark today. Perhaps he even read some of René's literature. Those works reveal René as polite and genteel—a nobleman's nobleman. His tournament rules penalize knights who've "spoken ill of the ladies."

With its lush, cupped blooms and full fragrance, 'René d'Anjou' echoes its namesake's romantic personality. It's a rose the Good King would have been proud to offer, along with a gentle kiss on the hand, to his favorite damsels.

Here's to late bloomers and survivors. Louis-Philippe d'Orléans (1773–1850), France's "Citizen King," was born at Paris's Palais Royale but spent the prime of his life in exile.

Louis-Philippe lived in a golden age of rose creation, and several of his country's hybridizers honored him with introductions after he was finally elected "King of the French" at age fifty-seven. Modeste Guérin, an award-winning plantsman also famous for his peonies and clematis, created a keeper with his 'Louis-Philippe' rose. Although richly colored, the rose's demure flowers recall a royal whose life taught him humility.

After distinguishing himself as a young military hero early in the French Revolution, Louis-Philippe deserted at age nineteen to escape the Reign of Terror. In Switzerland, he traveled under the name Mr. Chabos, taught school, and romanced a cook. In Scandinavia, he called himself Müller and seduced a housekeeper. Then came four transient years in America, a year in Cuba, and finally, more than a decade in England. (During this time, his father was executed, his mother was banished to Spain, his two brothers died of tuberculosis, and his dear sister, Adélaïde, married unhappily.)

A better life budded in 1809, when Louis-Philippe married Marie-Amélie of the Two Sicilies, an Italian princess who had also lived in exile. They started a large family in England, but returned to sumptuous living in France after Napoléon was defeated. By this time, Louis's Bourbon cousins held the French throne, and he recovered his fortune. When the July Revolution erupted, bourgeois politicians named Louis-Philippe France's first (and last, as it happened) "constitutional" monarch.

Liberal and humbled by his nomadic life, Louis-Philippe ditched the traditional crown, ermine capes, and gold-embroidered finery of the monarchy for plain military attire. His projects—such as turning the Palace of Versailles into a national museum— endeared him to the populace early on. But Louis-Philippe's position eventually went to his head; and when famine, high unemployment, and a financial crisis struck in 1848, the working classes revolted again. They trashed the Palais Royale and burned down the king's castle at Neuilly. In the fracas, Louis-Philippe and his queen—disguised as "Mr. and Mrs. Smith"—hailed a cab and fled to England. The ex-king died there, still in exile, two years later.

The rose 'Louis-Philippe' landed in America many years after its namesake but established stronger roots there. Lorenzo de Zavala, who visited Paris as Mexico's minister to France in 1834, brought the rose to his home in Texas just as that state declared its independence. 'Louis-Philippe' also found its way to the Bahamas and Florida, where it's such a commoner it's called the 'Florida Rose'. Some gardeners liken the rich fragrance of 'Louis-Philippe' to cherries, although its bud shape may be more true to its namesake's character: The lively, slightly conniving King Louis-Philippe was often portrayed in caricatures as a pear.

Louis-Philippe

TYPE: CHINA • INTRODUCED: 1834

PARENTAGE: UNKNOWN

Adélaïde d'Orléans

TYPE: RAMBLER • INTRODUCED: PRIOR TO 1829

PARENTAGE: UNKNOWN

Even in her old age, Louise Marie Adélaïde Eugénie d'Orléans dazzled the author James Fenimore Cooper. "I do not remember a more frank, intelligent, and winning countenance," he wrote. "She has little beauty left, except that of expression; but this must have made her handsome once, as it renders her singularly attractive now."

Her family's chief gardener, Antoine Jacques, must have also admired the mature Adélaïde. He named one of his very best rose creations after her. 'Adélaïde d'Orléans', displayed at the Orleans family garden at Neuilly, would have been a magnificent sight each June.

By this time in her life, Adélaïde had seen many Junes come and go. Raised in the Palais Royale and smartly tutored by the innovative Madame de Genlis, the teenage Adélaïde was exiled abruptly when the Reign of Terror began. Unable to return home from England, she fled with Madame de Genlis to Belgium and Switzerland, finding refuge with relatives. When she was about twenty-three, Adélaïde headed to America—but again, the going wasn't easy. Shipwrecked, she landed instead in Guadeloupe, West Indies, where she met and married the much older but wealthy German-American merchant George Casper von Schroeppel. Although they had a fine home, the love, if there was any, didn't last. When she was allowed to return to France in 1814, the thirty-seven-year-old princess went home alone, leaving George and their four children to fend for themselves. Thereafter, she styled herself Madame Adélaïde and became widely respected as her brother Louis-Philippe's closest advisor.

In a portrait made at about the same time as Jacques bred her namesake rose, abundant brunette curls frame Adélaïde's face. A hint of knowing sadness glimmers in her large, doelike eyes. Her taste in clothes was refined but simple. In its soft blush color, 'Adélaïde d'Orléans' exhibits similar elegance—slightly wistful, with buds that curve ever so graciously; tipping, like fate, with the wind.

Kronprinzessin Viktoria von Preussen

TYPE: BOURBON • INTRODUCED: 1887

PARENTAGE: SPORT OF 'SOUVENIR DE LA MALMAISON'

Although remembered by a German-bred rose with the German version of her name, crown princess Victoria of Prussia (1840–1901) may have been too British for her own good. Her parents, Queen Victoria and Prince Albert of England, groomed their oldest child to influence world politics. Victoria and Albert had high hopes for Germany's future when they married Vicky—as they called their remarkably intelligent daughter—to Crown Prince Friedrich Wilhelm of Prussia, fondly known as Fritz.

Instead, Vicky found herself hopelessly caught between Fritz's old-line, militaristic Hohenzollern family—who didn't trust her and rarely allowed her to travel—and a mother who demanded that she send home "court reports" every day. Vicky and Fritz's progressive ideas branded them as the black sheep of the German court.

A near mirror image of her short, plump mother, Vicky appeared oddly matched with the tall, dashing Fritz, but they were one of the nineteenth century's few truly happy royal couples. Although Fritz was often called away to battle, they devoted summers to a lifelong remodeling project updating the magnificent New Palace at Sanssouci, sometimes called the Prussian Versailles. Vicky, an accomplished painter and draftswoman, designed new, geometric gardens for the palace, with an artist's eye for detail. Always charitable, she also founded schools for girls and nurses.

In the late 1860s and early 1870s, as Prussia evolved into Germany, Fritz and Vicky patiently waited their turn to be the country's emperor and empress. Historians love to speculate about how different world events might have been if the enlightened Fritz hadn't died of throat cancer ninety-nine days after finally inheriting his father's throne. World War I was brewing, and Vicky was powerless after being evicted from her castle and shut out of German affairs by her coldhearted eldest son, Kaiser Wilhelm II, and the cunning Otto von Bismarck.

Following her mother's style, the forty-eight-year-old widow, now called the Empress Frederick, wore black for the rest of her life. But she always had sympathizers in the garden. The Berlin nurseryman Ludwig Späth named 'Kronprinzessin Viktoria' in appreciation for her support of the German Rose-Lovers Society. The Tea rose 'Kaiserin Friedrich', created in 1889 by Heinrich Drögemüller, also honored her.

Both roses were likely displayed at Friedrichshof, Vicky's private retirement estate near Frankfurt. Here, she designed an unabashedly English-style park: 160 acres with glass houses for her chrysanthemums, orchids, and gardenias; a naturalistic landscape of conifers through which Tea roses were allowed to climb; and 1,200 rose standards on terraces with rose-covered arcades. (Today, the mansion is a luxury hotel.)

Like the crown princess during her childbearing years, 'Kronprinzessin Viktoria' is a compact specimen rarely out of flower. (Vicky and Fritz had eight children, two of whom died young.) The rose's blossoms have a lemony urgency, like the letters Vicky wrote to her mother, in which she underlined every other word for emphasis. 'Kronprinzessin Viktoria' charms passersby with its lingering fragrance—quite befitting a royal who always liked to get in the last word.

Duchesse de Brabant

TYPE: TEA • INTRODUCED: 1857

PARENTAGE: UNKNOWN

Here grows the story of a petite, party-going princess who excelled at horseback riding Magyar style—astride, like a man—and later became a lonely, dispirited queen. At sixteen, Marie Henriette Anne von Habsburg-Lothringen (1836–1902) married the aloof, eighteen-year-old Léopold II, Duke of Brabant. Long before they became the queen and king of Belgium, notes one historian, they were like "a stable boy and a nun"—*she* being the stable boy, albeit one who loved music, literature, and art. (Queen Victoria of England, Léopold's cousin, found the duchess the "superior" of the pair.)

Belgians called the pretty Marie "the Rose of Brabant," so it's only fitting that she has a namesake in the garden. Somewhere, however, relatives of one Comtesse de Labarthe—for whom the rose was originally named—may be crying foul. H. B. Bernède of Bordeaux, the rose's hybridizer, or another politically astute nurseryman, may have presented it, rechristened, to the well-traveled Marie and Léo when they visited the French emperor Napoléon III.

President Teddy Roosevelt often wore the 'Duchesse de Brabant' as a boutonniere. His admiration was reciprocated in Belgium, where King Léopold kept an autographed picture of Roosevelt in his palace study. Marie, however, never cared much for politics or politicians—especially her husband.

Léo and Marie had four children, but their only son died before he was ten. The king consoled himself by building museums and parks, exploiting Africa's Congo, and chasing women in Paris. Marie, by then a stay-at-home queen, busied herself with charities and other pet projects. She filled her rooms at Laeken, the family's castle, with Belgian dogs, helping to make Laekenois shepherds, schipperkes, and Brussels griffons popular breeds. Also a fan of Belgian lace, she once lobbied fellow queens across Europe not to buy cheap imitations.

Meanwhile, family troubles multiplied. Léo and Marie's first two daughters, Louise and Stephanie, married unhappily, and Léo's sister, Charlotte, had a mental meltdown after a brief stint as empress of Mexico. In spite of the hardships of tending to them all, Marie remained handsome. The *New York Times* noted that even as an older woman, she kept her figure and "defied the ravages of time." She certainly knew how to pamper herself: Her favorite home was in Spa, a town famous for its healing waters.

'Duchesse de Brabant' honors her memory in its lovely, cupped blooms—a little youthful exuberance, a bit of quiet elegance, and a slight hint of superiority. (One might also imagine its droopy blooms, heavy on their stems, as the teenage duchess's full, pouffy skirts.) The rose's blush-pink color is as pure as its namesake's complexion. And with a whiff of its Tea-like fragrance, the passion swells. Hum a Hungarian gypsy melody when you partake of it, please—that was the duchess's favorite music.

Although almost nothing is known about the creation of 'Duchesse de Gramont', there's a good possibility it honors Ida d'Orsay (1802–1882), the wife of Antoine, the ninth duke of Gramont, a loyal subject of France's King Charles X. One of the country's oldest noble families, the Gramonts supplied a steady stream of ladies who could have been honored with roses. Ida's predecessors included the witty, ultrastylish Béatrice de Choiseul, an intimate of Madame de Pompadour's who lost her head at the guillotine in 1794, and the gorgeous Aglaé de Polignac, whose mother was one of Marie Antoinette's best friends. Aglaé escaped the Terror but died in 1803, at the age of thirty-five, in a house fire in Edinburgh.

The alluring Ida assumed the title of duchess in 1830, when she married Aglaé's oldest son. Her own family had its characters, too—among them the iconic dandy and artist Alfred d'Orsay, notorious for his relationship with the writer Margaret Gardiner, the British countess of Blessington. Margaret's 1841 memoir, *Idler in France,* which describes a visit with the Gramonts, is almost a paean to the warm, gentle, and elegant Ida, "unspoilt by all the brilliancy of her position." The countess paints a picture of an affectionate family led by the widowed grandfather Antoine VIII, who devoted much of his time "to the culture of flowers." Ida doted on her mother and grandmother, whose salon she often visited, "sparkling with diamonds, after having hurried away from some splendid fête at which she was the brightest ornament."

Riding in a swan-shaped sleigh with fur-covered seats and silver bells, Ida and Antoine inspired the countess to gush, "The Duchess, wrapped in a pelisse of the finest Russian sable, never looked handsomer . . . her fair cheeks tinged with a bright pink by the cold air, and her luxuriant silken curls falling on the dark fur that encircled her throat."

But in nineteenth-century France, the party never lasted long. By the next summer, with the July Revolution stirring, Ida had to show her courage when hecklers attacked her home in Paris. Loyal to the deposed King Charles X, the Gramonts went temporarily to Edinburgh. Ida lived to be eighty; she's buried in a rather grand, pyramidal tomb in Paris.

If ever a rose hinted at an opulent lifestyle, it's 'Duchesse de Gramont', with its profuse sprays of flowers and buds that recall the pink of Ida's cheeks. These open into lavish blossoms like layers of pearl-colored petticoats. The rose's scent is as heady as court gossip, well worth sidling up to for a bit of the day's juice.

Duchesse de Gramont

TYPE: NOISETTE • INTRODUCED: PRIOR TO 1836

PARENTAGE: UNKNOWN

Mme. Isaac Pereire

TYPE: BOURBON • INTRODUCED: 1881

PARENTAGE: UNKNOWN

S ometimes, a rose's name does double duty—especially when the woman it commemorates has a famous husband. Fanny Pereire (1825–1910) was clearly proud of her marriage to Isaac Pereire, one of nineteenth-century France's most successful financiers. Rather than asserting her independence the year after he died, she honored him—and herself as well—by paying the nurserymen Jules and Charles Margottin to introduce this rose as 'Mme. Isaac Pereire'.

Or perhaps Fanny simply wanted to differentiate her maiden and married names. You see, Isaac was the brother of her father, Emile Pereire. Today, such a marriage would raise eyebrows. But in the speculative, supercompetitive heyday of France's Second Empire, inseparable brothers Emile and Isaac apparently liked to keep it all in the family.

Although the Pereires worked for the Rothschilds early in their careers, animosities developed between the two families after the Pereires built their own railroad, the Paris–Saint-Germain line. Major contributors to the modernization of France, they also founded the first investment bank, the Crédit Mobilier (which crashed spectacularly); developed hotels and other opulent buildings in Paris's seventeenth arrondissement; built the first French steamship company to offer regular service to New York; and created a seaside resort at Achachon. It's said that Pereire-Rothschild tensions ran so deep that the stationmaster at Gretz-Armainvilliers—where both families had country estates—booked train times so that the business magnates didn't cross paths.

For all of their high style, the Pereires didn't live in a glamorous bubble. They helped lead the Saint-Simonian movement, which supported the rights of laborers. Isaac, who was awarded the Legion of Honor for his philanthropy, promoted his ideas through his own daily newspaper, *La Liberté;* he also established a generous prize for writing on social economics.

In a photograph taken during her later years, Mme. Isaac Pereire—sumptuously attired in silk, with her silver hair loosely atop her head—appears to be a good-natured, grandmotherly sort. Her namesake rose, in contrast, suggests her family's audacious nature. Its powerful scent, cherished as one of the most fragrant among Old Roses, comes at you with all the subtlety of—appropriately enough—an oncoming train.

Alice Belin du Pont (1872–1944) was no longer a youngster when she married, but her romance certainly had "explosive" qualities. Both her husband, Pierre, and her father headed companies that manufactured munitions, part of the vast DuPont industrial empire. First cousins Alice and Pierre shared a passion for gardening and music.

Their legacy, Longwood Gardens in Pennsylvania, remains one of America's grandest horticultural showplaces, with more than a thousand lushly landscaped acres. They dreamed it up even before they were married, during vacations in Italy and France in 1910 and 1913. While their travel companions shopped, Alice and Pierre toured landmark gardens at the Villa d'Este, Gori, Gamberaia, Vaux-le-Vicomte, and Courances for inspiration.

Pierre was the mastermind behind Longwood's huge twenty-garden conservatory, its acres of dancing fountains, and its open-air theater. Alice was the colorizer who kept it picture-perfect for parties and musical events, ordering plants from around the world. Her favorites were orchids, daylilies, irises, lilacs—and of course, roses. The du Ponts were active in the Garden Society of America and founders of the Orchid Society of America, among other horticultural groups.

'Mrs. Pierre S. du Pont' once had pride of place in one of the du Ponts' formal gardens alongside the salmon-colored 'Margaret McGredy', with a background of yews. Developed in France, Alice's rose was introduced to commerce by the Conard-Pyle Company, a nursery near Longwood. Letters that president Robert Pyle wrote to her suggest that not just any new Hybrid Tea would suffice for a lady with such discerning taste in plants. Pyle watched "yellow seedling 1277" for several seasons before naming it. "Up to this time," he wrote, "the writer has not had the opportunity of convincing himself that the rose is fully and unreservedly worthy of your name." Alice typed her permission the next day: "I beg to advise that I will be very glad to have the rose named after me."

She lives on elsewhere in the garden, too. The 1923 pink Canna Hybrid 'Mrs. Pierre du Pont', the 1962 pink Mandevilla 'Alice du Pont', and the 2005 white Cattleya orchid 'Alice B. du Pont' also honor her.

Alice's life, however, was not confined to country clubs and gardens. A graduate of Bryn Mawr College, she volunteered with the American Red Cross during World War I. In 1917, she founded her own charity, the Nileb Foundation. ("Nileb" is "Belin" spelled backwards.) She also supported the Philadelphia Orchestra and the Metropolitan Opera of New York.

A distinguished-looking brunette with a beautiful olive complexion, the always impeccably dressed Mrs. Pierre S. du Pont had a megawatt smile. Looking at her dynamite alter ego in the garden, one gets the feeling that it was contagious.

Mrs. Pierre S. du Pont

TYPE: HYBRID TEA • INTRODUCED: 1929

PARENTAGE: CROSS OF SEEDLINGS BRED WITH 'OPHELIA'

Sir Thomas Lipton

TYPE: RUGOSA • INTRODUCED: 1905

PARENTAGE: *ROSA RUGOSA* X 'CLOTILDE SOUPERT'

F ew sportsmen in history have been as successful at losing as Sir Thomas Lipton (1850–1931), who spent more than $5 million over thirty years trying to win the America's Cup yacht race. His payoff, aside from a conciliatory gold cup, was the deep-steeped admiration of the American tea-buying public.

His namesake rose, 'Sir Thomas Lipton', may also have been a consolation—or an enticement. Hybridized by the U.S. Department of Agriculture's Dr. Walter Van Fleet and introduced by the American nursery Conard-Pyle, it appeared during a year when Sir Thomas effectively canceled the America's Cup race because he disagreed with the rules. By then, the beloved Brit had tried and failed to win with a succession of yachts named *Shamrock I* through *Shamrock III*. In 1907, he tried again with *Shamrock IV*, and the year he turned eighty, he brought *Shamrock V* across the Atlantic. For his determination and exceeding good humor, he was deemed "the best of all losers" and awarded a gold trophy.

In business, Lipton was always golden. Born in Scotland to Irish parents, he stowed away to America as a teenager with $8. He returned to Glasgow five years later with $150, a rocking chair for his mother, and a head full of ideas for his first business, a grocery store. A savvy promoter, he paraded placard-bearing hogs through town and used his own jovial face in ads. By the time he was thirty, Lipton owned twenty stores—the seed of what became a six-hundred-store empire in England, America, and elsewhere. To supply his stores with affordable tea for the working classes, Lipton bought bankrupt plantations in Ceylon. His tea—sold in innovative, individualized tins—became a staple around the world.

He was friendly with King Edward VII and King George V, but his commoner background made Lipton more popular with wealthy Americans than with the British aristocracy. (He wasn't invited to join the Royal Yacht Squadron until he was nearly eighty years old.) Queen Victoria knighted him in 1898, but as one of his friends commented, "he didn't need to be knighted to be a nobleman." A lifelong bachelor (to the chagrin of many a hopeful woman), Lipton always had a soft spot for the poor, and willed most of his fortune to charitable projects in Glasgow.

Befitting his buoyant personality, 'Sir Thomas Lipton' is a rose of exceptional vigor. Its pure white blossoms recall both Lipton's good heart and his healthy head of white hair. But it may be most recognizable by its textured foliage—a shamrock-green reminder of the longtime yachtsman's ruddy, wind-whipped skin.

Lady Waterlow

TYPE: HYBRID TEA • INTRODUCED: 1902

PARENTAGE: 'LA FRANCE DE '89' X 'MME. MARIE LAVALLEY'

Before the infamous Wallis Simpson caused a constitutional crisis by marrying Prince Edward of England, the royal family received another American divorcée more warmly. Margaret Hamilton, Lady Waterlow (1849–1931), was reportedly "a great favorite with royalty," including Queen Victoria's daughter Princess Louise, the Duchess of Argyll.

Born in Iowa, where friends remembered her as Maggie, a "May-faced, morning-eyed" girl, she was the daughter of a well-to-do grocer who took his family to San Francisco in 1860 and built a banking fortune. Maggie grew up alongside the children of other wealthy Californians, including the Hearsts, Crockers, and Stanfords. Her friends stood by her after her first husband, a cad from Boston, squandered her inheritance and abandoned her. Those connections came in handy in the summer of 1881, when Sir Sydney Waterlow of Great Britain visited the Crockers' mansion.

An English baronet, publisher, and banking magnate, the recently widowed Sir Sydney had served as Lord Mayor of London. Although old enough to be Maggie's father, he clicked with her through ten days of horseback riding, bowling, and billiard playing. (Maggie is said to have been a pool shark.) Within months, Maggie had become Lady Waterlow, dazzling society at ever higher levels. Along with her title, a husband, and eight grown stepchildren, she gained a mansion in London, a country estate in Kent, and a villa in Cannes.

The Waterlows entertained lavishly, with Princess Louise and King Gustav V of Sweden among their frequent houseguests. The Waterlows also befriended Emperor Meiji of Japan, who invited them to his first-ever garden party for Westerners. A society writer in 1913 called Lady Waterlow "the real royal American," attributing her popularity to her discretion: "She never advertises herself, so that royals can come and go to her house with no publicity."

Generous philanthropists, the Waterlows bequeathed their twenty-nine-acre High-gate estate to the London County Council as a "garden for the gardenless." Containing ponds, gardens, an aviary, and the historic Lauderdale House, it's known today as Waterlow Park.

'Lady Waterlow' no doubt graced the gardens of the couple's villa in Cannes. The rose's creator, the handsome old Gilbert Nabonnand, designed lush landscapes for many of the aristocratic villas around the French Riviera, often using palms and other plants suited to the warm climate. Nabonnand introduced more than two hundred roses, and the dozens of Madames, Princesses, Duchesses, and Counts among them reflect his A-list of Riviera clients.

Although the delicate coloring of its blossoms blush with "May-faced" appeal, some may find it amusing that 'Lady Waterlow' is a modest Climber. The rose's pure form, however, is discreet—befitting the tasteful manners of the well bred and better married.

CHAPTER 4

*Storied
Characters*

WHERE BETTER TO RETELL A TALE OF LOVE
than in a garden? Rose creators have always been a literate bunch.
In the early years of cultivation, as neoclassicism blossomed, they
gave us a pantheon of sumptuous plants named for characters from
ancient mythology. Shakespeare's figures, equally timeless, have
also proved irresistible to many hybridizers. Then there are the
quirky roses named for heroines from Sir Walter Scott's swashbuckling novels, which are almost a breed unto themselves.

LÉDA
90

BELLE ISIS
92

DON JUAN
94

THISBE
96

PENELOPE
98

GREENMANTLE
100

FÉLICITÉ ET PERPÉTUE
102

OPHELIA
104

JULIA MANNERING
106

SOMBREUIL
108

Léda

TYPE: DAMASK • INTRODUCED: 1827

PARENTAGE: UNKNOWN

Greek mythology is full of famous couplings, but few of these stories have inspired such sensual art as Léda and the Swan, a tale about the seduction of the mortal queen Léda by the god Zeus, who disguises himself as a bird to win her sympathy.

In a rendering on classical Greek pottery, Léda rides calmly, clothed, on a large swan's back. Renaissance painters including Michelangelo, Leonardo da Vinci, and Antonio da Correggio often depicted her as a gloriously supple nude. The Victorian artist Gustave Moreau envisioned her as a helpless maiden under attack.

This isn't why her namesake rose is sometimes called 'Painted Damask', though— that's actually a reference to the flower's distinctive, picoteed color. But do those crimson touches imply an innocent blush or a sexy streak?

Legend has it that the day the swan seduced her, Léda also slept with her husband, King Tyndareus, and soon produced quadruplets. The half-immortal Helen and Pollux are said to be Zeus's offspring, while mortals Clytemnestra and Castor are King Tyndareus's. Helen's beauty provokes the Trojan War. Castor and Pollux end up in the sky as the constellation Gemini, while Clytemnestra grows up to lead a dysfunctional and murderous family. Léda's life doesn't exactly fly off the cheerful chart, either. In Euripides' drama, Léda is so shamed by her daughters' infidelities that she hangs herself.

Appropriately, 'Léda' is quite the drama queen of Old Rosedom. Its shapely buds curve gracefully, like the necks of cygnets. (One can almost imagine them dancing to Tchaikovsky.) They open into glorious blooms, which are both opulent and feather light. The rose's strong, sensuous fragrance could send anyone—even a high-ranking god—into a frenzied fit of love.

Was it this rose's distinctive myrrh fragrance that inspired the Belgian creator of 'Belle Isis' to name it after an Egyptian goddess? Perhaps.

Like other gentlemen of his era, Louis Parmentier (1782–1847) undoubtedly heard reports of the ancient sites being unearthed by European archaeologists along the Nile and elsewhere during his lifetime—including the large temple at Philae dedicated to Isis.

Parmentier was most fascinated, however, with roses. You might even call him one of horticulture's high priests. He belonged to a famous family of plantsmen and owned one of the largest gardens in Europe, with about 3,000 roses. Although more than 850 of those were his own creations, the intensely devoted Parmentier didn't seem to care much about sharing them. Most of his hybrids entered the market after he died.

Isis, the highest-ranking goddess in ancient Egypt's mythical universe, was the daughter of Nut (the mother of the sun, moon, and stars), the sister and wife of Osiris (the underworld ruler), and the mother of Horus (the sky god). Clever and protective, Isis represented fertility, immortality, and magic—the ultimate Earth mother. Her image, with her winged arms outspread to ward off evil spirits, often appears on ancient coffins.

Believed to be healers and dream interpreters, Roman-era priests and priestesses of Isis used roses in their apothecaries and worship services. Most likely, they utilized *Rosa gallica,* a popular medicinal plant and the rose from which all other Gallicas—including 'Belle Isis'—are descended.

'Belle Isis' gained its own measure of immortality after British rose breeder David Austin crossed it in 1961 with 'Dainty Maid'. Their offspring became 'Constance Spry', the first of Austin's wildly popular English Roses.

With one glimpse of the slightly crenellated petals of 'Belle Isis', it's clear something divine is going on. One of Parmentier's best roses, it has an unusually feminine color for a Gallica. The rose's beguiling scent is mysterious, too—some might say magical, even. Sacrifice your senses to its charms, and 'Belle Isis' could transport your imagination to the land of papyrus and palms.

Belle Isis

TYPE: GALLICA • INTRODUCED: 1845

PARENTAGE: UNKNOWN

Don Juan

TYPE: LARGE-FLOWERED CLIMBER • INTRODUCED: 1958

PARENTAGE: 'NEW DAWN' SEEDLING X 'NEW YORKER'

The legend of the lusty rogue Don Juan has inspired playwrights, composers, and poets for more than 350 years. But no one named a rose for him until 1958. Perhaps there just wasn't a blossom seductive enough, or a rose breeder daring enough, until then.

"Heaven offended, laws violated, girls led astray, families dishonored, relatives outraged, wives ruined, husbands driven to despair"—Don Juan wreaks havoc everywhere, usually pursued by someone he's wronged. He fears no one, including God. He's a callous but charismatic libertine who seduces every woman he meets and is eventually dragged to hell. Oh, yes, and he's not above murder.

From the Age of Reason to the Romantic Era and into the twenty-first century, artists have tweaked the story of Don Juan to reflect the mood and philosophy of their times. He first appeared in 1630, in the moralistic comedy *El Burlador de Sevilla y convidado de piedra* (The Trickster of Seville and the Stone Guest), by the Spanish monk Tirso de Molina. Jean-Baptiste Molière's famous version, with a wicked commedia dell'arte sensibility, was censored soon after its 1665 premiere in Paris and wasn't seen again in France for about two hundred years because it glorified rational thinking and anarchy.

By the 1790s, eight operas about Don Juan—including Mozart's timeless *Don Giovanni*—had been staged. Then came Lord Byron's mock epic poem *Don Juan* (1821); plays by Aleksandr Pushkin (*The Stone Guest*, 1830), Alexandre Dumas (*Don Juan de Marana*, 1831), José Zorrilla (*Don Juan Tenorio*, 1844), and George Bernard Shaw (*Man and Superman*, 1903); and the tenderhearted 1995 film *Don Juan de Marco*.

As wonderful as all of these versions are, poetry and opera can't provide the same tactile sensuality as the rose garden's 'Don Juan', hybridized in Italy and named when it was introduced in America by Jackson and Perkins. To surrender to its pleasures, plant it near a trellis and let your mind roam wherever its canes and delicious, Damask-like fragrance take you. Or caress the undersides of its velvety, ruffled petals, which are intoxicatingly dark and dangerous-looking.

Pyramus and Thisbe, beautiful young lovers from Babylonia, have a tragic story similar to that of Shakespeare's Romeo and Juliet—with an added element of garden lore. Although this young couple were next-door neighbors, their parents wouldn't allow them to marry. Meeting every night, they couldn't touch; they were only able to exchange whispers and notes through a crevice in the wall that separated their homes.

One night they agreed to meet in a nearby field, where a spring flowed near a mulberry tree with white berries. Thisbe arrived first. As she waited, a lioness with a bloody mouth came to the spring to drink. Thisbe hid behind a rock, dropping her veil—which the lioness picked up and stained.

When Pyramus arrived and saw the lioness with the bloody veil, he thought Thisbe had been eaten. Horrified, he stabbed himself. Blood flowed into the earth, turning the tree's fruit deep red. Thisbe emerged, saw the berries, and thought she was lost. When she spotted the wounded Pyramus, she gave him his first—and last—kiss as he died in her arms. Then she plunged Pyramus's sword into her breast, imploring the tree, "Let thy berries still serve for memorials of our blood." Thus, ever since, mulberries have been red.

Inexplicably, the rose that commemorates Thisbe is a creamy yellow. Perhaps its creator, the British rosarian Reverend Joseph Hardwick Pemberton, simply wanted to convey that love is pure and slightly golden.

Pemberton, who died in 1926, became a professional rose breeder after a career as a cleric with the Church of England. He had a soft spot for classical antiquity, also naming roses for Daphne, Danae, Ceres, Penelope, Galatea, Clytemnestra, and Callisto. He invented the Hybrid Musk class of roses to produce hardy, continuously blooming plants that would thrive in England. He once told a visitor, "Do not approach these plants with a knife in your hand. They'll resent it."

Given its namesake's sad business with a sword, it's not hard to see why 'Thisbe' would resent pruning. The rose's nubile buds are as becoming as a lovely young woman's figure. And its small, informal blossoms speak of the innocent but somewhat reckless nature of youth, especially in matters of love.

Thisbe

TYPE: HYBRID MUSK • INTRODUCED: 1918

PARENTAGE: 'MARIE-JEANNE' X 'PERLE DES JARDINS'

Penelope

TYPE: HYBRID MUSK • INTRODUCED: 1924

PARENTAGE: 'TRIER' X 'OPHELIA'

In 1818, the great French hybridizer Jean-Pierre Vibert created a 'Pénélope' as pink as grenadine. In the 1960s, a modern 'Penelope'—a red Tea with an ivory center—crept into gardens. In between came the lone surviving 'Penelope'—this exquisite Hybrid Musk by the British author and rosarian Reverend Joseph Hardwick Pemberton.

What character could possibly inspire so many variations? The beautiful, wily wife of the hero Odysseus in Homer's *The Odyssey*. Like her counterparts in the garden, the literary Penelope came by her name rather awkwardly: It's derived from the Greek word *penelops,* which means "duck." As the myth goes, her father threw her as a newborn into the sea because he'd wanted a son. She was saved by ducks.

Although they were madly in love, Penelope and Odysseus spent twenty years apart while Odysseus fought the Trojans, Cyclops, Circe, Sirens, and Calypso. Lamenting his absence day and night, the faithful Penelope cried for years. But this didn't make her a shrinking violet. For three years, the cunning Penelope used her weaving skills to fend off all the chieftains who wanted to marry her and take Odysseus's land. She couldn't wed again, she insisted, until she'd sewn a death shroud for her father-in-law, Laertes, who was still alive. But what Penelope wove each day, she unraveled each night.

When the suitors discovered her trickery, they ate her livestock, drank all of her wine, and seduced her maids. Just in time, an old stranger arrived and restored order. Everyone except for the ever-practical Penelope—who must have had a poor memory and bad eyesight—thought Odysseus had returned, in disguise. To test him, Penelope ordered Odysseus's bed moved to another room. The stranger bellowed that it couldn't be done, since he'd built his bed from a live olive tree. She flung her arms happily around his big neck, and they lived for a long time after.

The apricot-pink buds of 'Penelope' blossom into ivory beauties with just a hint of blush, suggesting the slight embarrassment of being caught in an act of deception, however noble. Their gorgeous color also recalls the ambrosial complexion said to have been endowed upon the mortal Penelope by the goddess Minerva as she slept. But don't think of this rose as sweet; its musky fragrance exudes strength, maturity, and a shrewd nature.

Greenmantle

TYPE: EGLANTINE • INTRODUCED: 1895

PARENTAGE: UNKNOWN

The British hybridizer James Plaisted Wilde, Lord Penzance (1816–1899), brought one of Sir Walter Scott's most intriguing female characters to life—in the garden, at least—with this rose. It commemorates the beautiful "unknown enchantress" in the novel *Redgauntlet,* which debuted in 1824. Until well along in the story, the protagonists, Darsie Latimer and Alan Fairford, know her only by the nickname they've given her, Greenmantle.

Borrowing from history, the story is set on the border of England and Scotland in the eighteenth century as a few Jacobites, loyal to the usurped Stuart dynasty, are plotting to retake the British throne from King George III and the Hanoverians. Then fiction steps in. Scott's Jacobite leader, Sir Hugh Redgauntlet, plans to kidnap his long-lost nephew—Darsie—to increase the Jacobites' manpower. Redgauntlet is thwarted, however, by his captive niece, Lilias, who was separated from Darsie when she was an infant. Concealing herself in a fancifully embroidered green cape, she sets out to warn her unsuspecting brother. Luckily for both of them, Scott also supplies help in the character of the handsome lawyer Alan Fairford—along with a colorful cast including a Quaker, a sea captain, and the blind fiddler Wandering Willie.

The rose's vivid color is a perfect reminder of Greenmantle's cheeks—which turn "crimson with a deep blush" when she's in a room with Alan or Darsie. The attraction is mutual: Both men are jelly-kneed when they're around her. "Plague on her green mantle, she can be nothing better than a fairy; she keeps possession of my head yet," Alan says after Lilias has slipped out of his office without telling him her name.

The rose that commemorates her has a similar effect on gardeners, especially on humid mornings when its green apple–like fragrance—mysteriously held in the cloak of its leaves—perfumes the air.

Talk about twice as nice. 'Félicité et Perpétue' is one of very few roses named for two people. For this, we can thank Mrs. Antoine A. Jacques. Her husband, the duke of Orléans's head gardener at Neuilly-sur-Seine in the early 1800s, held off naming a rose he'd developed to commemorate the birth of a child his wife was carrying. Then, surprise! Mrs. Jacques had twin girls.

Some rosarians believe Jacques named the twins after Saints Felicity and Perpetua. A pious act on Jacques's part, perhaps, but not exactly the kind of story one would expect to inspire a garden of delights. The young noblewoman Vibia Perpetua and her slave Felicitas died gruesomely, martyred at Carthage in 203 A.D. after refusing to give up their Christian faith.

Perpetua's written record of their prison experience, *Acta*, may be the oldest surviving text by a Christian woman. Documenting her preparation for martyrdom, part of it describes her mystical frenzy: She dreamed of a bronze ladder to heaven, spiked with weapons on its sides and a serpent at the bottom; at the top she saw a white-haired shepherd with his flock in a glorious garden.

Perpetua and Felicitas, resolute in their passion, left young children behind. (The pregnant Felicitas worried that she wouldn't give birth in time to be martyred with her friends, since the law forbade killing pregnant women. But the group prayed together, and three days before the execution, Felicitas had a daughter.) The women sang in ecstasy as they entered the Colosseum to be mauled by a fierce cow and killed by gladiators.

Some experts, citing the rose's listing as 'Félicité-Perpétue' in nineteenth-century catalogs, think Jacques could have intended its name to mean, simply, "perpetual happiness." In full bloom, it can certainly inspire euphoria. With perfectly formed rosettes along its rambling stems, this rose celebrates spring like a cheerleader waving her pom-poms. Get close enough, and her primrose scent might even move you to rapture.

Félicité et Perpétue

TYPE: RAMBLER • INTRODUCED: 1827

PARENTAGE: *R. SEMPERVIRENS* X 'NOISETTE'

Ophelia

TYPE: HYBRID TEA • INTRODUCED: 1912

PARENTAGE: SEEDLING OF 'ANTOINE RIVOIRE'

O rose of May! Has literature ever produced a more analyzed young woman than the deliciously mad maiden of William Shakespeare's *Hamlet*? We think not, judging by the volume of popular psychology books her character has spawned. And paintings, too—especially by the pre-Raphaelites, who were enthralled by her waifish, virginal aspects. Even our own era's singer-songwriters can't resist her; she's inspired Natalie Merchant, the Indigo Girls, and Kate Bush, among others.

So it's no surprise that Ophelia also found her way into the garden as one of more than 150 roses bred by the Englishman William Paul (1822–1905), who was also a prolific writer of horticultural books. Naming many of his early plants for British royalty, he later favored authors and their characters.

Ophelia must have been one of Paul's favorites, since he gave the name to a rose he knew was a milestone. With her elegant, conical buds, 'Ophelia' set the stage for the perfect form of all Hybrid Teas. As she opens, her slightly larger outward petals reflex gracefully, hinting at the literary persona who came unraveled.

Shakespeare's Ophelia had the misfortune to believe that Hamlet, the doomed and gloomy prince of Denmark, loved her. Ignoring the warnings of her father and brother not to respond to Hamlet's advances, she lost her mind after he brushed her off with the famous line "Get thee to a nunnery."

Her nonsensical rambling aside, Ophelia knew the language of herbs and flowers: "There's rosemary, that's for remembrance; pray, love, remember: and there is pansies, that's for thoughts," she said as she wove garlands absently before drowning herself. Artists often depict her floating in a glassy stream strewn with those garlands. She didn't carry roses, perhaps because Shakespeare didn't find them as sinister as crow-flowers, nettles, and "dead men's fingers," as orchids were called.

Borne on long, erect stems, Paul's refined 'Ophelia' has all the grace you would expect of a refined young noblewoman. And yet, in its satiny, opalescent blooms, there's a touch of our heroine's fragile, ephemeral nature—the quiet inward glow of a lovelorn maiden.

Julia Mannering

TYPE: EGLANTINE • INTRODUCED: 1895

PARENTAGE: UNKNOWN

This pretty rose, like the fictional character it brings to the garden, is stronger than its delicate-as-porcelain petals might imply. It grows on a tall, super-prickly bush sometimes recommended as a "defensive" hedge.

The elderly British hybridizer James Plaisted Wilde, Lord Penzance (1816–1899), introduced 'Julia Mannering' a few years before he died. His friend Gertrude Jekyll once suggested that Lord Penzance occupied himself with "the happy marriage of roses" as a salve after many years of practicing divorce law. Certainly a man with a romantic streak, Lord Penzance named all but a few of his roses after characters in Sir Walter Scott's swashbuckling historical novels. He must have especially liked the novel *Guy Mannering*, since he found inspiration there for 'Julia Mannering', 'Lucy Bertram', and 'Meg Merrilies'.

Guy Mannering's plot involves the fate of Harry Bertram, the heir to an ancient Scottish manor in the 1780s, an uneasy period when gypsies, smugglers, colorful farmers, landed gentry, and corrupt officials all crossed paths. Kidnapped at age five, Harry has grown up believing he's Vanbeest Brown, a lowly merchant's son. He's in love with Julia Mannering, whose wealthy father forbids the young couple to see each other.

Julia and her father, followed by the lovestruck Brown, have returned to Scotland after many years in India. Quite a pill, Julia has a quixotic nature. She's proper, but not above sneaking out at night to rendezvous with her boyfriend.

The rose 'Lucy Bertram' commemorates Harry's smart and sensitive sister, who stands to lose the manor if her long-lost brother isn't found. 'Meg Merrilies' honors the novel's ill-fated Amazonian gypsy—Harry's guardian angel—who orchestrates a resolution.

In spite of their bookish nature, Lord Penzance's roses—known as Eglantine Hybrids—are slightly stranger than fiction. They were created from species Eglantines—the wild sweetbriar roses native to England. Thus, you may find only traces of the fresh-apple fragrance of 'Julia Mannering' in its blossoms. The rose keeps its true scent, like a secret love letter to Vanbeest Brown, demurely stashed in its foliage.

It's not hard to see why several hybridizers would commemorate Marie-Maurille Virot de Sombreuil (1774–1823) with roses. Legend has it that this heroine of the French Revolution drank a glass of blood to prove her loyalty to the cause and save her aristocratic father's head.

She's still drawing blood, so to speak, among rosarians who've spent years sorting out her multiple identities in the garden. 'Sombreuil', a Climber, first appeared in the United States in 1959, although it may have been bred much earlier in France. It's not to be confused with 'Mlle. de Sombreuil', a less spectacular Bourbon Tea created in about 1850 by the hybridizer known only as Monsieur Robert. And according to rosarian Stephen Scanniello, yet another 'Sombreuil'—an Alba—existed in the 1820s.

The real Mlle. de Sombreuil was the daughter of Charles-François Virot, the marquis of Sombreuil, who had the misfortune of being the royalist governor of Les Invalides, Paris's huge military infirmary, in 1792. As revolutionaries executed other nobles by the thousands, Marie and her two brothers landed in prison with their father.

The story goes that when the marquis was brought to trial, young Marie pleaded for mercy, agreeing to drink to the Revolution's success if the court would spare her father's life. "We hate aristocrats!" she cried, according to an 1837 history by Thomas Carlyle. Whether the cup actually contained blood or just vile red wine is debatable, although the incident also found its way into works by Victor Hugo, Jacques Delille, and Ernest Legouve.

And alas, Mlle. de Sombreuil's stunt only postponed the inevitable. Her father and one of her brothers eventually lost their heads at the guillotine. Her other brother survived prison only to be executed later for fighting against the revolutionary forces. Marie eventually returned to a noble life, marrying the Count of Villelume and living to be forty-nine. Her heart is kept alongside those of other heroes of French history in the crypt at Les Invalides.

Given her history, isn't it curious that all three roses honoring Mlle. de Sombreuil are white? Perhaps their creators focused on her pure intentions. The huge, creamy blooms of 'Sombreuil' seem to be wide-eyed with innocence. But try to enjoy its lemon-apple scent up close, and a thorny attitude emerges. Careful, or those prickles will have you screaming bloody murder.

Sombreuil

TYPE: LARGE-FLOWERED CLIMBER • INTRODUCED: PRIOR TO 1959

PARENTAGE: UNKNOWN

CHAPTER 5

Well-Bred
Ladies
& Gents

WHAT COULD BE MORE STIMULATING THAN SHARING an occasional pot of compost tea with roses named for history's most influential plantsmen and women? Their stories open a window into the evolution of gardening. And while hybridizers' wives, daughters, and mothers may have not been celebrities in the nineteenth and early twentieth centuries, they're prominently present in the garden now: It was a smart *rosariste* who named his finest creations for his loved ones.

F. J. LINDHEIMER
112

JAMES VEITCH
114

LADY BANKS
118

CHAMPNEYS' PINK CLUSTER
120

WILLIAM LOBB
122

FORTUNE'S DOUBLE YELLOW
124

RHODOLOGUE JULES GRAVEREAUX
126

MRS. B. R. CANT
128

GRAHAM THOMAS
132

GERTRUDE JEKYLL
134

F. J. Lindheimer

TYPE: SHRUB • INTRODUCED: 2000

PARENTAGE: 'CAREFREE BEAUTY' X 'BAYSE'S BLUEBERRY' SEEDLING X 'RISE 'N SHINE'

Ferdinand Jacob Lindheimer (1801–1879), an early American naturalist, discovered hundreds of plant species during nearly a decade of collecting in the nineteenth century.

Lindheimer's name appears on dozens of native Southwestern plants, including varieties of prickly pear cactus, gaura, goldenrod, and daisies. Horticulturalist G. Michael Shoup, whose Antique Rose Emporium gardens are near Lindheimer's South Texas stomping grounds, thought gardeners could use one more. Shoup named one of his first Pioneer Series roses after the man who's often called the father of Texas botany.

Like other liberal Germans of his era, the well-educated Lindheimer came to America in the 1830s as a political refugee. He collected plants and insects in Mexico, fought in the Texas Revolution, and tried truck farming. Finally, he found steady work selling specimens of unknown Texas flora to his friend George Engelmann (the founder of the Missouri Botanical Garden) and Harvard University botanist Asa Gray.

Although Lindheimer wasn't the first or only plant collector in Texas, he was the first to live there permanently. And because he spoke English, Spanish, and German—as well as communicated with the native peoples—he also became a community leader. In 1844, Prince Carl of Solms-Braunfels called on Lindheimer to help find a settlement for his colonists. Thus came to be the town of New Braunfels, near San Antonio. When the prince paid Lindheimer with property, the plantsman's collecting days ended. Lindheimer married, raised four children, founded a school, served as justice of the peace, and published the town's German-language newspaper.

Lindheimer's modest house, restored in the 1960s but virtually unchanged, now draws tourists in New Braunfels. Although the botanical garden Lindheimer envisioned never materialized, a local plant society keeps a nice native garden there, featuring plants Lindheimer discovered.

The rose 'F. J. Lindheimer' has as sturdy a pioneer spirit as its namesake. Its young blooms, vivid as a Texas sunset, age gracefully to a color that makes them worthy of being considered a true (if new) "yellow rose of Texas."

I n the cutthroat world of Victorian horticulture, exotic orchids could make or break a business. And no one had better access to them than the Englishman James Veitch Sr. (1792–1863), the first commercial nurseryman to send his own plant collectors overseas.

Veitch practically sprouted with sap in his veins, the second patriarch in a dynasty whose history paralleled a century's worth of gardening fashions. His father, John Veitch, was the head gardener at Killerton estate when the landed gentry wanted forests. John launched one of England's first large-scale tree companies; a four-thousand-acre forest he planted at Killerton still stands. So does an eighteen-acre Killerton flower garden that John and James created for the next generation, when more ornamental landscapes became de rigueur.

Expanding the business, the canny James built his reputation as a grower of dahlias, American plants, and exotics. But he made history in the 1840s, dispatching plant-hunting brothers William and Thomas Lobb to opposite ends of the world to supply his greenhouses with rare plants. No quick jaunts, these three-year expeditions were an expensive gamble. But they paid off.

Imagine the excitement, in a greenhouse guarded like Fort Knox, as James Veitch and Son—now including his eldest son, James Jr.—unpacked their first alstroemeria, echites vine, oncidium orchid, red salvia, and dipladenias from Brazil. By 1851, only the Royal Botanic Gardens at Kew had more new plants than the Veitches.

In the late nineteenth century, rare orchids were a wealthy gentleman's status symbol. In addition to hiring plant hunters, the Veitches also employed the world's first orchid hybridizer to develop new varieties. James Jr. took the business to London, building state-of-the-art greenhouses that coddled plants with varying climate needs.

The Veitches also sold roses, including English and French varieties. Their namesake rose, 'James Veitch', introduced by the French hybridizer Eugène Verdier, came to commerce shortly after James Sr. died. Most likely, the Verdiers and Veitches traded nursery stock. Although the story of the rose's naming is lost, 'James Veitch' was chosen by someone with a discerning eye. Modern expert Gregg Lowery says it's one of the greatest roses ever introduced.

Contemplating the purplish blossoms of 'James Veitch', you might easily see a horticultural society blueblood with a feverish, passionate nature. Alternatively, you might also be reminded of the rare blue *Vanda caerulea,* an orchid that Thomas Lobb collected for the Veitches in India. The stems of 'James Veitch' have irregular, dagger-sharp prickles. Wrap your fingers around one, and you'll have a good sense of what it was like to deal with the thorny James Jr.

James Veitch

TYPE: MOSS • INTRODUCED: 1864

PARENTAGE: UNKNOWN

Lady Banks

TYPE: CHINA • INTRODUCED: 1807
PARENTAGE: UNKNOWN

In the late 1700s, few women on earth had a life as modern as that of Lady Dorothea Hugessen Banks (1758–1828), wife of the influential Sir Joseph Banks. She and Sarah Sophia Banks, Sir Joseph's devoted sister, were his constant travel companions—an erudite, inseparable, and childless family.

It's a special woman who will allow jars of pickled rodents in her living room. But Dorothea couldn't afford to be squeamish: Her Soho Square home served as London's first natural history museum, also housing a vast herbarium and library that she and Sophia helped catalog. Sir Joseph, in his younger years, had traveled on Captain Cook's epic voyage around the world, amassing specimens, drawings, and curiosities at every stop. He entertained the world's scientific cognoscenti several times a week as founder of the Royal Gardens at Kew and president of the Royal Society. (One of his favorite amusements would be shocking today. Sir Joseph owned scales—a novelty then—and judiciously recorded his visitors' weights.)

The apolitical Bankses counted both King George III and Benjamin Franklin among their friends. They often entertained at their country manor, Spring Grove, where they kept a large botanic garden, kangaroos, and merino sheep. (Sir Joseph helped build England's wool industry.) Near Revesby, Sir Joseph's ancestral home, they hosted an annual fishing party. In between all of this activity, the Bankses traveled nonstop.

Dorothea, a comely, orphaned heiress sixteen years younger than her husband, had personality to spare. Chatty, with an easy laugh, she wrote breathlessly to friends about her "much unsettled" life, which was only slightly dampened by Sir Joseph's painful bouts of gout. She loved company. "We shall have much satisfaction in some comfortable casino parties together," she coaxed one friend. (She must have been a good gambler; she attended races faithfully.)

And Lady Banks loved diamonds and dishes. "A little china mad," as her good-natured husband once described her, she loaded her dairy barn with one of the world's finest collections of porcelain and china. This was madness, however, that Sir Joseph encouraged: For one of their anniversaries, he penned an essay about the history of china, had it lavishly illustrated, and presented it to his wife as a gift. He also wrote poems to her.

The botanist Robert Brown, one of many plant hunters the Bankses supported, named *Rosa banksia*—popularly known as 'Lady Banks'—upon discovering it in China. Needless to say, the white variety grown at Spring Grove was as pampered as its namesake. The long, arching canes of 'Lady Banks' are busy with delicate little blossoms. The lively, somewhat lacy display—especially in its sunny yellow form, 'Lutea'—blooms well before some other flowers, like an invitation to the joyful party of spring.

Champneys' Pink Cluster

TYPE: NOISETTE • INTRODUCED: 1802

PARENTAGE: 'OLD BLUSH' X *ROSA MOSCHATA*

Few people would consider the American Revolution a war of the roses. But the events of 1776 played a surprising role in rose history. Had he not lost his property, South Carolinian John Champneys (1743–1820) might never have created the West's first repeat-blooming rose.

Until the Revolution, Charles Town—now Charleston—hummed with wealthy, satisfied British subjects. Champneys, born in South Carolina to a British official, owned one of Charleston's large wharfs. But he spent much of 1776 jailed with other prominent citizens deemed to be British sympathizers. In legal papers he filed, he complained about being "dragged about from jail to jail," threatened with execution, and finally exiled. The "rebel" government confiscated his property and his business and subjected his family "to many insults, inconveniences and hard usage."

Champneys took his family away for a decade, and after his first wife died, his next marriage was politically expedient: He wed Amarinthia Lowndes, a daughter of one of South Carolina's first governors.

Rebuilding his reputation, Champneys bought a rice plantation on the Wallace River in 1796. According to David Ramsay's *History of South Carolina,* the twenty-six-acre spread boasted one of the South's most elaborate gardens, including six acres with "sheets of water," abundant with fish; a ten-acre "pleasure ground" where native trees, shrubs, and flowers bloomed alongside more exotic plants from Europe, Asia, and Africa; and orchards that produced pears and pecans.

Champneys also tinkered here with roses. In about 1802, he "fertilized" a white Musk with pollen from the China 'Old Blush'. The first hybridization of a rose in America, it produced a new variety with abundant clusters of smallish, slightly double, pale pink blooms. Most sensationally, like its China parent, the rose bloomed for much of the year—a quality French hybridizers had yet to achieve.

Champneys shared seedlings with the Long Island nurseryman William Prince as well as with his neighbor, the French immigrant nurseryman Philippe Noisette. While Prince introduced the rose as 'Champneys' Pink Cluster', Noisette used it as a parent for the similar 'Blush Noisette'—which he sent home to his brother Louis, a famous Parisian nurseryman. 'Blush Noisette' landed in Empress Joséphine's garden at Malmaison, where Redouté painted it and a botanist christened it *Rosa noisettiana*. Thus began a rose revolution; by 1825, French breeders had created more than thirty-five new roses of the "Noisette" class.

G. Michael Shoup of the Antique Rose Emporium calls the musky fragrance of 'Champneys' Pink Cluster' "one of the sweetest perfumes in the rose world." It has one of the prettiest little blooms, too, flowering in profuse clusters almost nonstop. It's said that Champneys' orchard produced fruits in succession from May to October. But of course—how else could the trees compete with his lovely roses?

William Lobb

TYPE: MOSS • INTRODUCED: 1855

PARENTAGE: UNKNOWN

While other collectors gathered seeds and dried specimens for Great Britain's national collection, William Lobb (1809–1864) sent back living plants and seeds to be propagated and sold commercially by his boss, James Veitch Sr. Lobb, a talented amateur botanist from Cornwall, caught the travel bug working as a gardener near the port town of Falmouth, where trading ships from exotic locales often docked. His brother, Veitch worker Thomas Lobb, helped William land his first overseas assignment and soon found himself overseas as well. While William scoured Chile, Peru, Ecuador, California, and Oregon for treasures, Thomas plumbed the forests of Indonesia, the Philippines, and other points east.

The brothers faced perils such as yellow fever, dysentery, uncooperative natives, and broken bones. Getting exotic plants back to England alive made for dicey business, too. William once spent a year replacing four cases of plants from the Andes Mountains after a Peruvian warehouse owner let the first batch perish. On ships, delicate plants could succumb to saltwater spray, rough seas, and careless seamen. And if they survived all that, they could freeze waiting to be unloaded at the English docks.

William, not always detail oriented, could be smitten by scent: One historian mentions a primrose he sent home with only the note "The whole air for a considerable distance was perfumed with it." And his poor handwriting and labeling sometimes gave his employers fits.

Of the many woody shrubs and conifers he sent to Europe, one in particular sparked the ire of American botanists. In 1853, after the Americans showed him a giant Sequoia under study in California, the faithful British subject rushed home with seeds. The Americans intended to name the tree *Washingtonia gigantea,* after George Washington; but English botanists beat them to it, registering the famous giant Sequoia as *Wellingtonia gigantea,* in honor of the famous British general.

The prolific French nurseryman Jean Laffay bred 'William Lobb' during the explorer's lifetime. Most likely, however, Lobb never saw it. He'd disappeared into California's gold rush country by then, much to the consternation of his employer. Some historians believe Lobb caught syphilis on his travels. He spent his last three years in San Francisco, sending seeds to Kew Gardens instead of his boss. He never returned home.

Thankfully, his namesake rose is more dependable. Rose lovers appreciate 'William Lobb' for its generous clusters of mossy buds—which it "ships out" faithfully for a long period each summer. Like the redolent primrose William enjoyed in the wild, the rose's strong scent can fill a room. Close your eyes, inhale, and imagine a romantic journey.

Those who enjoy a cup of afternoon Darjeeling or Earl Grey tea can be glad the intrepid Scottish plant hunter Robert Fortune (1812–1880) penetrated the hostile territory of China in the 1840s, after the British won the Opium Wars. He wore native dress and learned to speak Mandarin so he could smuggle the secrets of tea making across the Himalayas to India and Ceylon, where the British broke China's monopoly on their must-have beverage.

Fortune's first expedition to China, in 1843, involved less espionage but no less cunning. Collecting unknown plants for the Horticultural Society, he always carried small optical instruments as enticements. Such gifts enabled him to send home rare species "which were only found in the gardens of the rich, and which, of course, were not for sale," he wrote in *Three Years' Wanderings in the Northern Provinces of China* (1847), the first of several books documenting his adventures. The Society especially wanted peaches from the Emperor's garden and blue-flowered peonies. Fortune was just as thrilled to find a new rose in Ningpo.

"On entering one of the gardens on a fine morning in May, I was struck with a mass of yellow flowers which completely covered a distant part of the wall," Fortune wrote in that first book. "The color was not a common yellow, but had something of buff in it, which gave the flowers a striking and uncommon appearance. I immediately ran up to the place, and, to my surprise and delight, found that it was a most beautiful new double yellow climbing rose." He sent cuttings home, and the rose became known in the West as 'Fortune's Double Yellow'. Its Chinese name, 'Wang-gang-ve', means "yellow rose."

Returning to the Orient several times over a 20-year period, Fortune introduced about 120 new plants to the West, including various azaleas, lilies, rhododendrons, bonsai, and a second rose that bears his name. 'Fortuniana', a white blooming Climber, is a favored rootstock plant for breeding roses today in the South.

His books—including *A Journey to the Tea Countries of China* (1852), *A Residence Among the Chinese* (1857), and *Yedo and Peking* (1863)—were popular, too, giving curious Europeans a compelling insider's glimpse of China's customs, language, landscape, tea making, and botanical riches. (Fortune even explained how to handle chopsticks.) Some historians find it odd that his books don't mention his wife and his children, who saw very little of him when they were young.

Fortune may have charmed his way into Chinese gardens, but he also had a take-charge personality. Once, while weak from a fever, he single-handedly fended off a pirate attack with his double-barreled fowling piece and two pistols. 'Fortune's Double Yellow' likewise has a complex personality: Its salmon and apricot blooms are deeper after a cold winter. Fortune himself noted the rose's color variations, which he thought added greatly to the plant's beauty and character.

Fortune's Double Yellow

TYPE: CHINA • INTRODUCED: 1845

PARENTAGE: UNKNOWN

Rhodologue Jules Gravereaux

TYPE: TEA • INTRODUCED: 1908

PARENTAGE: 'MARIE VAN HOUTTE' X 'MME. ABEL CHATENAY'

You might not be reading this book if Madame Jules Gravereaux hadn't convinced her husband to give up his first hobby in the late 1800s. In the "living museum" that Jules Gravereaux (1844–1916) ultimately created, he preserved from extinction hundreds of Old Roses that we still enjoy. Especially notable were the nineteenth-century Gallicas, which were losing ground all over France to newer classes of roses that bloomed more than once a year.

The origin of 'Rhodologue Jules Gravereaux' shows just how widely his effort was appreciated. ("Rhodologue" is a now-obsolete term that means "rose scientist.") The rose was created in Brazil by the Portuguese professor and writer Joaquim Fontes, one of Gravereaux's many international friends. Fontes probably presented the rose to Gravereaux as a gift.

An executive with Paris's Bon Marché department store, Gravereaux had retired, wealthy, in his forties. Buying a five-acre estate in Val-de-Marne in 1892, he immersed himself in the art of photography. Madame Gravereaux, apparently not liking all the hours her husband spent in the darkroom, encouraged him to try a pastime that involved fresh air. He obliged by planting a rose in the kitchen garden.

Clearly a type A personality, Gravereaux soon owned about sixteen hundred varieties of roses, began hybridizing them, and became his era's leading authority on rose history. He hired landscape designer Edouard André to create a "roseraie"—the world's first garden devoted entirely to roses, with every type systematically displayed, classified, and labeled. By 1902, Gravereaux's famous Roseraie de L'Haÿ contained about four thousand varieties of cultivated roses and nine hundred species, or wild, roses. By 1910, the garden had swelled to eight thousand varieties—all the known roses of the time—and also featured a museum, a library, and a laboratory. The Italian writer Gabriele d'Annunzio, among the many international visitors, voiced his approval of the garden's abundance. "In love, one needs excess," he said. (Owned by the French government since 1937, the Roseraie remains a tourist attraction. While much hasn't survived, the three thousand or so extant plants include many extremely rare specimens.)

Gravereaux also helped plan the rose gardens at the Château de Bagatelle in Paris's Bois de Boulogne park and re-created Empress Joséphine's rose collection at Malmaison.

Years ago, Gallicas and other Old European roses were often referred to as "Pinks" because many of them had pink flowers. The bloom color of 'Rhodologue Jules Gravereaux', therefore, is a spot-on tribute. As is its intense fragrance. Gravereaux was so keen on scent, he bred Rugosa roses for perfume oil.

Mrs. B. R. Cant

TYPE: TEA • INTRODUCED: 1901

PARENTAGE: UNKNOWN

During the 1880s and 1890s, Benjamin Revett Cant was the king of exhibition roses in England. His nursery's catalogs prominently featured his championship trophies from the National Rose Show and other competitions. One year, he reportedly won fifty-four first prizes in a month.

Cant had a trophy wife of sorts, too—Elizabeth Pettitt Cant, twenty-four years his junior. She gave him seven children, assuring future generations to continue the family business, which began in southeast England around 1765.

Early in his career, Ben Cant sold trees, American plants, greenhouse plants, bulbs, and seeds. He began specializing in roses in the 1850s. And when his nephew, Frank Cant, audaciously opened a competing rose nursery nearby, an unfriendly rivalry took root. Tensions between the two were said to be so intense that mail addressed simply to "Mr. Cant" in Colchester was returned with a postcard forcing the sender to choose one or the other.

In the early twentieth century, both Cants participated in Colchester's high society—hosting dinner and shooting parties, going "beagling," and playing tennis, golf, and cricket. One has to wonder if gossip flew after Frank introduced his Hybrid Perpetual 'Mrs. Frank Cant' in 1899 and Ben, perhaps to steal some of that thunder, answered with the Tea rose 'Mrs. B. R. Cant' and the Hybrid Perpetual 'Ben Cant'.

According to the family lore, it simply took a long time before Ben raised a seedling worthy of Elizabeth. As dutiful in the garden as its namesake was at home, 'Mrs. B. R. Cant' won several major awards, including the National Rose Society's gold medal. Unfortunately, Ben didn't live to enjoy the accolades; he died, in his early seventies, in 1900. His son Cecil put the rose into commerce.

After Cecil died, his wife, Mildred—who deserved a rose, too, but never had one named for her—ran the company until 1959. Eight years later, the family's two factions finally made up, merging to become Cants of Colchester. They produced one of the world's most popular roses, the buff-colored Hybrid Tea 'Just Joey', in 1972. Curiously, they no longer grow any of the family namesakes, which may not have been great garden performers in England.

'Mrs. B. R. Cant', however, acclimated just fine across the pond, where she has long been a commanding presence in Southern gardens. Her opulent blossoms are generously cupped—each a coveted winner in its own right, and exceptionally fragrant, redolent of Tea and Damask.

Graham Thomas

TYPE: SHRUB • INTRODUCED: 1983

PARENTAGE: 'CHARLES AUSTIN' X 'ICEBERG' SEEDLING

The British garden designer Graham Stuart Thomas (1909–2003) was a gentleman of propriety. He insisted that head gardeners at the estates where he worked call him "Mr. Thomas." He never missed teatime. He ate meals at appointed hours and retired early each night. "There was a fixity of purpose about all he did whether he was working, entertaining or relaxing," writes John Sales in the foreword to Thomas's last book. "Not for him the aimless dreaming of the romantic or the impulsive fecklessness of the spendthrift."

Except, of course, when it came to Antique Roses. Thomas was among the twentieth century's most influential plantsmen and one of England's first "period planters." Working for the National Trust, which preserves historic properties, he oversaw and restored at least sixty large landscapes. Abundant Old Roses usually wound their way into Thomas's designs—regardless of whether they were actually appropriate—a point that sometimes drew criticism from period purists.

Thomas's romantic side also flourished in the many gardening books he wrote and illustrated. In *The Complete Flower Paintings and Drawings of Graham Stuart Thomas,* he channeled John Keats, noting a "wonderful moment, during a pause in a too-busy life, when the flower before us reveals its glory afresh, unsullied, and the truth of beauty bursts upon us." He often incorporated quotes from his favorite poets and used music-related anecdotes in his books. (For example, he considered dark-colored flowers necessary "bass notes" in a garden.)

During his early career in commercial nurseries, Thomas liked retreating to his desk on winter evenings. In later years, he simply found writing relaxing. Drawing and painting with watercolor, too, served as an escape. In one book, he described making pen-and-ink drawings of winter flowering plants while he was "fire-watching during World War II."

Given Thomas's passion, it was only natural that his longtime friend, the hybridizer David Austin, invited him to pick a namesake rose that would keep his spirit alive. "In the field full of seedlings from which we chose this, there were very few yellows, and none with so rich and deep a colour," Thomas wrote in his *Rose Book*. "The only rose that in any way approaches its rich tint of apricot in the bud is 'Lady Hillingdon'," he added. (This was another of his favorites.)

Thomas's ashes were scattered at his garden masterpiece, the National Collection of roses at the thirteenth-century Mottisfont Abbey in Hampshire—so he is still, in a sense, cultivating Mottisfont's blooms each June. And of course, 'Graham Thomas' is among the three hundred roses grown there. Visitors to the garden are requested not to smoke—perhaps in deference to Thomas, who so hated the habit that he kept a "no smoking" sign in his car. He had an "acute and discerning" sense of smell. That may be another reason he chose this rose, which possesses a rich Tea scent.

Gertrude Jekyll

TYPE: SHRUB • INTRODUCED: 1986

PARENTAGE: 'WIFE OF BATH' X 'COMPTE DE CHAMBORD'

The word "profusion" could have been invented to describe the abundant look of the gardens Gertrude Jekyll (1843–1932) designed. Flowers billowing in borders, spilling over pergolas, climbing into trees, covering mounded shrubs, decorating doorways—all came together in her "cottage" style, executed on a grand scale.

Miss Jekyll, as she was fondly called, didn't hide her disdain for anything too garish or purple. In her description of a showy crimson Rambler, one can almost hear the uppity attitude: "Those of us whose eyes are trained to niceties of colour-discrimination wish that the tint of this fine flower had been just a shade different." Nor did she allow plants such as azaleas and rhododendron to romp together; their colors clashed.

In honoring her with one of his early English Roses, David Austin wisely chose a plant with a brilliant pink bloom. Miss Jekyll—who gathered about eleven thousand flowers each spring to make potpourri for her home at Munstead Wood—counted scent among a rose's most important properties. Appropriately, Austin believes 'Gertrude Jekyll' has the finest, strongest Old Rose–like fragrance of any of his introductions.

Although she appears primly Victorian in some photographs, Miss Jekyll grew up as an Arts and Crafts–period diva. Spending hours in her father's workshop, she mastered "country crafts" such as carpentry, metalworking, carving, and embroidery. Über-craftsman William Morris knew the prominent Jekylls, as did the essayist John Ruskin and the author Robert Louis Stevenson (who borrowed their name for his novel *Dr. Jekyll and Mr. Hyde*).

With her father's encouragement, Gertrude painted quite well. In her thirties, dogged by weak eyesight, she switched to a larger canvas—the great outdoors. Her plantings were as dense as the intricate patterns of Morris's textile designs, with harmonious colors, textures, lines, and shapes contributing to a complete "picture." The sought-after Miss Jekyll created more than four hundred gardens in Great Britain, Europe, and the United States, often working with the architect Sir Edwin Lutyens. She also ran a successful garden center, and somehow found time to write and take photographs for gardening books and magazines.

Although she devoted a chapter of her 1902 book, *Roses,* to floral arrangements, Miss Jekyll disliked stiff, exhibition-style Hybrid Teas. Her vases, like her gardens, overflowed with lush, romantic Antiques. The full-figured blooms of Austin's 'Gertrude Jekyll'—as generously sized as their namesake—would have been a perfect addition to the mix.

Acknowledgments

WE'RE DEEPLY GRATEFUL TO THE MANY FRIENDS WHO HELPED THIS PROJECT BLOSSOM.

G. Michael Shoup supported every stage of our efforts, giving us studio space along with blooms from the display and mail-order gardens at his Antique Rose Emporium. Also contributing roses and advice were Gregg Lowery of Vintage Gardens, whose encyclopedic catalog was an important tool; Mel Hulse and the staff of the San Jose Heritage Rose Garden; Bob and Marcia Roenigk of the Vintage Rosary; Suzanne Longley of Suzanne Longley Landscapes; and Catherine Focke.

Brent Dickerson's books were indispensable references, and his responses to questions were unfailingly kind, witty, and insightful. Help with research materials also came from Colvin Randall at Longwood Gardens, Carolyn Barry of the New Braunfels Conservation Society, the South Carolina Historical Society, David Austin Roses, Cants of Colchester, the Natural History Museum in London, Cornell College, Elizabeth Bonnetot, and Tom Oxford.

Our agent, Joelle Delbourgo, and editor, Aliza Fogelson, guided us smoothly, cheerfully, and professionally through our first book publishing experience.

Bart Darling, Doug Gobel, and AZ Lab aided with digital image production, while Lisa Rebori at the Houston Museum of Natural Science organized the exhibit of photographs from the book. Sincere thanks also to graphic designers Mark Geer and C. Randall Sherman for their proposal ideas and inspiration; to the *Houston Chronicle;* and to our family, for their patience and understanding—especially Penny and Roland, for keeping us going with all those "desperate" meals.

Growing Old-Fashioned Roses

While Antique Roses are known for their sturdy natures, many factors affect their growth—including climate, sunlight, and soil conditions. Generally, Old European types such as Damasks, Gallicas, and Centifolias tend to flourish in colder environments, while Chinas, Noisettes, and Teas perform best in temperate zones. The guide here is approximate; consult a local nursery for the best varieties for your area. The dates given denote the year each rose was introduced.

KEY TO GROWTH HABITS

O	Once-blooming	C	Climber
R	Remontant	L	Large (*seven feet or larger*)
FF	Highly fragrant	M	Medium (*five to seven feet*)
F	Moderately fragrant	S	Small (*under five feet*)

ROSES FOR COLD CLIMATES (ZONES 4 THROUGH 6)

'Anaïs Ségalas', Centifolia, 1837 (O/FF/M)
'Belle Isis', Gallica, 1845 (O/FF/S)
'F. J. Lindheimer', Shrub, 2000 (R/F/S)
'Fantin-Latour', Centifolia, c. 1900 (O/FF/M)
'Goethe', Moss, 1911 (R/F/L)
'Greenmantle', Eglantine, 1895 (R/F/L)
'Henri Martin', Moss, 1863 (O/FF/L)
'Jacques Cartier'/'Marchesa Boccella', Hybrid Perpetual, 1868 (R/F/S)
'Jeanne d'Arc', Alba, 1818 (R/FF/L)
'Julia Mannering', Eglantine, 1895 (R/F/L)
'Léda', Damask, 1827 (O/FF/M)
'Omar Khayyám', Damask, 1893 (O/FF/L)
'Redouté', Shrub, 1992 (R/FF/M)
'René d'Anjou', Moss, 1853 (R/FF/M)
'William Lobb', Moss, 1855 (O/F/L)

ROSES FOR "FOUR SEASONS" CLIMATES (ZONES 6 THROUGH 8)

'Adélaïde d'Orléans', Rambler, prior to 1829 (O/F/C)
'Captain Thomas', Large-Flowered Climber, 1938 (R/F/L)
'Cardinal de Richelieu', Hybrid China, 1840 (O/FF/S)
'Champneys' Pink Cluster', Noisette, 1802 (R/F/L)

'Constance Spry', Shrub, 1961 (O/FF/C)
'Don Juan', Large-Flowered Climber, 1958
(R/F/L)
'Excellenz von Schubert', Hybrid Musk,
1909 (R/F/L)
'F. J. Lindheimer', Shrub, 2000 (R/F/S)
'Fantin-Latour', Centifolia, c. 1900
(O/FF/M)
'Félicité et Perpétue', Rambler, 1827
(O/F/C)
'Gertrude Jekyll', Shrub, 1986 (R/FF/L)
'Graham Thomas', Shrub, 1983 (R/F/L)
'Henri Martin', Moss, 1863 (O/FF/L)
'Jacques Cartier'/'Marchesa Boccella',
Hybrid Perpetual, 1868 (R/F/S)
'James Veitch', Moss, 1864 (R/FF/S)
'Jeanne d'Arc', Alba, 1818 (R/FF/L)
'Kronprinzessin Viktoria von Preussen',
Bourbon, 1887 (R/F/S)
'Mme. Eugène E. Marlitt', Bourbon, 1900
(R/FF/L)
'Mme. Isaac Pereire', Bourbon, 1881
(R/FF/L)
'Mozart', Hybrid Musk, 1937 (R/F/L)
'Mrs. Pierre S. du Pont', Hybrid Tea, 1929
(R/F/M)
'Penelope', Hybrid Musk, 1924 (R/F/M)
'René d'Anjou', Moss, 1853 (R/FF/M)
'Robin Hood', Hybrid Musk, 1927 (R/F/L)
'Sir Thomas Lipton', Rugosa, 1905
(O/FF/L)
'Sombreuil', Large-Flowered Climber,
prior to 1959 (R/FF/L)
'Thisbe', Hybrid Musk, 1918 (R/F/L)
'William Lobb', Moss, 1855 (O/F/L)

ROSES FOR TEMPERATE CLIMATES (ZONES 7 AND ABOVE)

'Archduke Charles', China, prior to 1837
(R/FF/M)

'Captain Thomas', Large-Flowered Climber,
1938 (R/F/L)
'Champneys' Pink Cluster', Noisette, 1802
(R/F/L)
'Duchesse de Brabant', Tea, 1857 (R/FF/M)
'Duchesse de Gramont', Noisette, prior to
1836 (R/FF/L)
'Excellenz von Schubert', Hybrid Musk,
1909 (R/F/L)
'F. J. Lindheimer', Shrub, 2000 (R/F/S)
'Fortune's Double Yellow', China, 1845
(O/F/C)
'Graham Thomas', Shrub, 1983 (R/F/L)
'Jacques Cartier'/'Marchesa Boccella',
Hybrid Perpetual, 1868 (R/F/S)
'Lady Banks', China, 1807 (O/F/C)
'Lady Waterlow', Hybrid Tea, 1902
(R/FF/C)
'Lamarque', Noisette, 1830 (R/FF/C)
'Louis-Philippe', China, 1834 (R/F/M)
'Mme. Eugène E. Marlitt', Bourbon, 1900
(R/FF/L)
'Mme. Isaac Pereire', Bourbon, 1881
(R/FF/L)
'Mozart', Hybrid Musk, 1937 (R/F/L)
'Mrs. B. R. Cant', Tea, 1901 (R/F/L)
'Mrs. Pierre S. du Pont', Hybrid Tea, 1929
(R/F/M)
'Napoléon', China, c. 1835 (R/FF/M)
'Ophelia', Hybrid Tea, 1912 (R/F/M)
'Penelope', Hybrid Musk, 1924 (R/F/M)
'Rhodologue Jules Gravereaux', Tea, 1908
(R/F/M)
'Robin Hood', Hybrid Musk, 1927 (R/F/L)
'Rubens', Tea, 1859 (R/FF/S)
'Sombreuil', Large-Flowered Climber, prior
to 1959 (R/FF/M)
'Souvenir de Victor Hugo', Tea, 1885
(R/FF/L)
'William Lobb', Moss, 1855 (O/F/L)

Resources

THE ANTIQUE ROSE EMPORIUM
www.antiqueroseemporium.com
800.441.0002

ASHDOWN ROSES
www.ashdownroses.com
864.468.4900

CHAMBLEE'S ROSE NURSERY
www.chambleeroses.com
800.256.7673

GARDEN VALLEY RANCH
www.gardenvalley.com
707.795.0919

HEIRLOOM ROSES
www.heirloomroses.com
503.538.1576

HIGH COUNTRY ROSES
www.highcountryroses.com
800.552.2082

ROGUE VALLEY ROSES
www.roguevalleyroses.com
541.535.1307

VINTAGE GARDENS
www.vintagegardens.com
707.829.2035

To Learn More

AMERICAN ROSE SOCIETY
www.ars.org
318.938.5402

HELPMEFIND
www.helpmefind.com/roses

THE HERITAGE ROSE FOUNDATION
www.heritagerosefoundation.org

Further Reading

Algrant, Christine Pevitt. *Madame de Pompadour: Mistress of France.* New York: Grove Press, 2002.

Aminrazavi, Mehdi. *The Wine of Wisdom: The Life, Poetry and Philosophy of Omar Khayyam.* Oxford, U.K.: Oneworld, 2005.

Austin, David. *The English Roses.* Portland, Oreg.: Timber Press, 2006.

Bamford, Francis, ed. *Dear Miss Heber: An Eighteenth Century Correspondence.* London: Constable and Company Ltd., 1937.

Barry, D. H., and James Chastain. *Encyclopedia of 1848 Revolutions.* Athens, Ohio: www.ohiou.edu, 2005.

Belkin, Kristin Lohse. *Rubens.* London: Phaidon Press Limited, 2005.

Bennett, Anna, tr. *Roses for an Empress: Joséphine Bonaparte and Pierre-Joseph Redouté.* London: Sidgwick & Jackson, 1983.

Browning, Oscar. *Goethe: His Life and Writings.* New York: Haskell House, 1972.

Carter, Harold B. *Sir Joseph Banks, 1743–1820.* London: British Museum (Natural History), 1988.

Champneys, John. *An Account of the Sufferings and Persecution of John Champneys.* London: 1778.

Christopher, Thomas. *In Search of Lost Roses.* Chicago: University of Chicago Press, 1989.

Copeland, Linda L., and Allan M. Armitage. *Legends in the Garden.* Atlanta, Ga.: Wings Publishers, 2001.

Coxhead, Elizabeth. *Constance Spry: A Biography.* London: William Luscombe Publisher Limited, 1975.

Dickerson, Brent C. *The Old Rose Adventurer.* Portland, Oreg.: Timber Press, 1999.

——. *The Old Rose Advisor,* vol. 1, 2d ed. Lincoln, Nebr.: Authors Choice Press, 2001.

——. *The Old Rose Index.* Lincoln, Nebr.: Authors Choice Press, 2001.

——. *The Old Rose Informant.* Lincoln, Nebr.: Authors Choice Press, 2000.

——. *Roll Call: The Old Rose Breeder.* Lincoln, Nebr.: Authors Choice Press, 2000.

Erickson, Carolly. *Josephine: A Life of the Empress.* New York: St. Martin's Press, 1998.

Fitzgerald, Edward. *Rubáiyát of Omar Khayyám.* New York: Hartsdale House, 1932.

Fortune, Robert. *Three Years' Wanderings in China.* London: Mildmay Books, 1987.

Hamilton, Edith. *Mythology: Timeless Tales of Gods and Heroes.* New York: New American Library, 1969.

Hardman, John, tr. *Memoires de Louis-Philippe.* New York: Harcourt Brace Jovanovich, 1977.

Harkness, Jack. *The Makers of Heavenly Roses.* London: Souvenir Press, 1985.

Harkness, Peter. *The Rose: An Illustrated History*. Ontario, Canada: Firefly Books, 2003.

Haslip, Joan. *Madame Du Barry: The Wages of Beauty*. North Yorkshire, U.K.: Tauris Parke Paperbacks, 2005.

Heriz-Smith, S. "The Veitch Nurseries of Killerton and Exeter c. 1780–1863: Part II." *Garden History* 16, no. 2 (1988).

Hugo, Victor. *Les Misérables*. New York: Signet Classic, 1987.

Jekyll, Gertrude, and Edward Mawley. *Roses*. North Stratford, N.H.: Ayer, 1983.

Jones, Colin. *The Cambridge Illustrated History of France*. New York: Cambridge University Press, 2003.

Keays, Etheyln Emery. *Old Roses*. New York: Earl M. Coleman, 1978.

Keefe, Simon P., ed. *The Cambridge Companion to Mozart*. New York: Cambridge University Press, 2003.

Leary, Francis. *The Golden Longing: A Portrait of the Turbulent Fifteenth Century and Its Immortals*. New York: Scribner's, 1959.

Lever, Evelyne. *Madame de Pompadour*. New York: St. Martin's, Griffin, 2000.

Lowery, Gregg, and Phillip Robinson. *Vintage Garden Book of Roses*. Sebastopol, Calif.: Vintage Gardens, 2006.

Lucie-Smith, Edward. *Henri Fantin-Latour*. New York: Rizzoli, 1977.

Martin, Clair G. *100 Old Roses for the American Garden*. New York: Workman, 1999.

Martin, Henri. "Martin's History of France: The Age of Louis XIV." *North American Review* 100, no. 207 (1865).

Melograni, Piero. *Wolfgang Amadeus Mozart: A Biography*. Chicago: University of Chicago Press, 2006.

Molière, Jean-Baptiste. *Tartuffe and Other Plays*. New York: Signet Classics, 1967.

New Braunfels Conservation Society. "Ferdinand J. Lindheimer, 1801–1879."

Nicholas, J. H. *A Rose Odyssey*. New York: Doubleday, Doran & Company, 1937.

O'Brian, Patrick. *Joseph Banks: A Life*. Boston: D. R. Godine, 1993.

Packard, Jerrold M. *Victoria's Daughters*. New York: St. Martin's, Griffin, 1998.

Pakula, Hannah. *An Uncommon Woman: The Empress Frederick*. New York: Simon & Schuster, Touchstone, 1995.

Parada, Carlos. *Genealogical Guide to Greek Mythology*. Philadelphia, Pa.: Coronet Books, 1993.

Phillips, Roger, and Martyn Rix. *Best Rose Guide*. Ontario, Canada: Firefly Books, 2004.

———. *The Quest for the Rose*. New York: Random House, 1993.

Quest-Ritson, Charles and Brigid. *The American Rose Society Encyclopedia of Roses*. New York: Dorling-Kindersley, 2003.

Ramsay, David. *The History of South Carolina, from Its First Settlement in 1670, to the Year 1808*. New York: David Longworth, 1809.

Robb, Graham. *Victor Hugo: A Biography.* New York: W.W. Norton & Company, 1997.

Robin Hood Project, The, www.lib.rochester.edu.

Rosa Gallica: A French Journal About Roses. Spring 2005, Autumn 2005, Spring 2006.

Rosa Mundi: Journal of the Heritage Rose Foundation. Autumn 2005, Winter 2006, Spring/Summer 2006, Autumn 2006, Winter 2007.

Scott, Walter. *Guy Mannering.* New York: Penguin Classics, 2003.

——. *Redgauntlet.* New York: Penguin Classics, 2000.

Shackelford, Geoff. *The Captain: George C. Thomas Jr. and His Golf Architecture.* Farmington Hills, Mich.: Gale Group, 1997.

Shephard, Sue. *Seeds of Fortune: A Gardening Dynasty.* London: Bloomsbury, 2003.

Shepherd, Roy E. *History of the Rose.* New York: MacMillan, 1954.

Shoup, G. Michael. *Roses in the Southern Garden.* Brenham, Tex.: Antique Rose Emporium, 2000.

Spry, Constance. *Flower Decoration.* Chicago: Academy Chicago Publishers, 1993.

Steen, Michael. *The Life and Times of the Great Composers.* Oxford, U.K.: Oxford University Press, 2004.

Steen, Nancy. *The Charm of Old Roses.* Washington, D.C.: Milldale Press, 1966.

Thomas, Graham Stuart. *The Complete Flower Paintings and Drawings of Graham Stuart Thomas.* New York: Harry N. Abrams, 1987.

——. *The Graham Stuart Thomas Rose Book.* Sagaponack, N.Y.: Sagapress, 1994.

——. *Recollections of Great Gardeners.* London: Frances Lincoln, 2003.

Von Goethe, Johann, Johann Peter Eckermann, and J. K. Moorhead, eds. *Conversations of Goethe.* Cambridge, Mass.: Da Capo Press, 1998.

Welch, William C. *Antique Roses for the South.* Boulder, Colo.: Taylor Trade, 2004.

Wilkins, Sophie, tr. *King René's Book of Love.* New York: G. Braziller, 1975.

Wimmer, Clemens Alexander. "Victoria, the Empress Gardener, or the Anglo-Prussian Garden War, 1858–88." *Garden History* 26, no. 2 (1998).

Wright, Allen W. "The Search for a Real Robin Hood," "Wolfshead Through the Ages," and "Interviews in Sherwood," www.boldoutlaw.com, 1997–2004.